the driving people

Selling your car

How to make your car look
great and sell it faster

Also from Veloce Publishing –

Caring for your bicycle – How to maintain & repair your bicycle (Henshaw)
Caring for your car – How to maintain & service your car (Fry)
Caring for your scooter – How to maintain & service your 49cc to 125cc twist & go scooter (Fry)
Dogs on wheels – Travelling with your canine companion (Mort)
Electric Cars – The Future is Now! (Linde)
First aid for your car – Your expert guide to common problems & how to fix them (Collins)
How your car works – Your guide to the components & systems of modern cars, including hybrid & electric vehicles (Linde)
How your motorcycle works – Your guide to the components & systems of modern motorcycles (Henshaw)
Land Rover Series I-III – Your expert guide to common problems & how to fix them (Thurman)
Motorcycles – A first-time-buyer's guide (Henshaw)
Motorhomes – A first-time-buyer's guide (Fry)
Pass the MoT test! – How to check & prepare your car for the annual MoT test (Paxton)
Roads with a View – England's greatest views and how to find them by road (Corfield)
Roads with a View – Scotland's greatest views and how to find them by road (Corfield)
Roads with a View – Wales' greatest views and how to find them by road (Corfield)
Simple fixes for your car – How to do small jobs for yourself and save money (Collins)
Selling your car – How to make your car look great and how to sell it fast (Knight)
The Efficient Driver's Handbook – Your guide to fuel efficient driving techniques and car choice (Moss)
Walking the dog – Motorway walks for drivers and dogs (Rees)
Walking the dog in France – Motorway walks for drivers and dogs (Rees)

www.rac.co.uk
www.veloce.co.uk

This publication has been produced on behalf of RAC by Veloce Publishing Ltd. The views and the opinions expressed by the author are entirely his own, and do not necessarily reflect those of RAC. **Please do not undertake any of the procedures described in this book unless you feel competent to do so, having first read the full instructions.**

First published in May 2012 by Veloce Publishing Limited, Veloce House, Parkway Farm Business Park, Middle Farm Way, Poundbury, Dorchester, Dorset, DT1 3AR, England. ISBN: 978-1-845844-50-9 UPC: 6-36847-04450-3

Fax 01305 250479/e-mail info@veloce.co.uk
web www.veloce.co.uk or www.velocebooks.com.

Readers with ideas for automotive books, or books on other transport or related hobby subjects, are invited to write to the editorial director of Veloce Publishing at the above address.
British Library Cataloguing in Publication Data – A catalogue record for this book is available from the British Library.
Typesetting, design and page make-up all by Veloce Publishing Ltd on Apple Mac.
Printed in India by Imprint Digital Ltd.

Selling your car

How to make your car look great and sell it faster

Nigel Knight

Contents

Contents

Introduction

If you're planning to sell your car, following this guide will improve your chances of making a quick sale and/or getting a decent price. Alternatively, if you're keeping your motor, this book will show you how to return it to a condition which should fill you with pride. Eight detailed yet concise chapters are packed with step-by-step cleaning methods and other advice to put the sparkle back into your car, injecting fresh pleasure and zest into driving and ownership.

This book isn't about using the disreputable tricks of rogue salesmen, of course, or ripping people off. Instead, simple techniques and expert skills, developed during more than 20 years of trading cars, will help you to present your car properly, which could earn you a significant amount more than you would get from a private sale with the car still in a tatty state, or by trading it in as a part-exchange. Hopefully, your car won't end up sitting on your drive for

months on end, being shown to a string of disinterested prospective buyers.

The book explains how to give your car – be it a family runaround, a luxury limousine, a top of the range sports model, or your cherished first motor – a stunning makeover, transforming its appearance to boost its sale value. Note, though, that it may not be suitable for vintage or other very old cars.

If you don't want to part with your car, you can use this guide to give it a first-class clean and a new lease of life; it can be the next best thing to buying a new car.

A detailed, top-to-bottom clean can make a startling difference to a car, and so, given that this is so important, I've included two chapters on the interior, and two on the exterior. It's best to start, in my experience, with the inside.

The book also covers the psychology of cleaning cars to sell them – why you should clean the car, not just the how to it – and gets in the minds of both the buyer and the seller to show how seemingly innocuous factors – such as wearing an overly-smart suit/string vest, the presence of a barking dog, or speaking on a mobile phone – can make or break a deal.

Although it delves a little into the psychology, most of the book is concerned with practical techniques, while top tips highlight particular aspects of specialist knowledge, and more than 100 pictures illustrate cleaning methods, restoring paintwork, and the importance of taking good photographs. There's advice on mechanical and electrical repairs, advertising, and sales techniques, including choosing a test drive route.

The methods outlined here aren't the only way to rejuvenate your car, but they are cost-effective. A bar of soap will be used for many tasks, rather than a shopping basket full of chemical sprays, foams and other finishers, so your clean should be environmentally-friendly, easy-to-do, and not burn a hole in your pocket. Some basic tools will be required: for example, two or three paintbrushes, a bucket, a microfibre cloth, a hose with a brush attachment, a nailbrush, a couple of toothbrushes, and a wet-and-dry vacuum cleaner (though the latter can be borrowed or hired). The full wet clean inside is crucial to get the best results, but should only be done with a wet-and-dry machine.

If you can't get hold of a wet-and-dry vacuum cleaner you can do a limited wet clean together with the brush-and-vac technique outlined in chapter two. This will give a better finish than vacuum-cleaning alone, though it won't be as good as a full wet clean.

Having the right equipment is important. **Note:** Using inappropriate, worn or badly fitting tools could damage your car, and make your work harder, and result in injury. You may already have many of the items in your home. Some, however, like the wet-and-dry vacuum cleaner, could prove to be a useful purchase for years to come. However, bear in mind whether any expenditure is money wisely spent.

Most chapters open with a list of tools and equipment required, your goal, the estimated time to complete the specific task, and – for people selling their car – a sale-booster rating out of five to indicate the impact that your work could have. Obviously, the sale-booster rating and the cleaning time can vary from car-to-car, depending on condition and age, but you should get a rough idea of the importance of each task for preparing a car for sale.

Before you start cleaning or doing anything else to your car, read the top tips, safety advice and warnings, as these could save you a lot of heartache and time. You may end up with the cleanest upholstery in the land, but you'll be kicking yourself if you've ruined your electrics by using too much water as you scrubbed away.

With patience, hard work, and the new skills gained from reading this book, your car's personality will soon shine through, giving you a great sense of satisfaction.

Well, that's enough talk. Let's get going; and ... good luck!

one
Nuts and bolts

Kit
Hose, car cleaning hose attachment brush, microfibre cloth, tea towel or chamois leather, tape.

Estimated time: 30 minutes.
Goal: Inspection to check for major repairs that may be required.
Sale booster factor: ☆ to ☆☆☆

TOP TIP: Carefully plan the order in which you'll carry out work on your car. You may be brimming with enthusiasm to get on with the job, but you can waste a great deal of time smartening up a car only to discover it needs to go to a garage or bodywork shop for repairs, and may return in desperate need of a second clean.

Inspection
Before cleaning your car, carry out an inspection to identify major mechanical, electrical or bodywork problems that should be addressed at the outset.

Assess all faults before deciding on which should be rectified. Not all faults are deal-breakers, especially on older cars, and it may not make economic sense to have them all repaired. For example, some people will still buy a car with worn but legal tyres, or if there are a few stonechips and scratches in the paintwork. After all, they're buying a secondhand car, which will inevitably have wear and tear.

Caution! If you have any safety concerns, with regard to brakes, tyres, suspension, warning lights, steering, or other parts, then they should be addressed. The same applies, obviously, if you're keeping your car.

Mechanics
Cars which have been regularly serviced and undergone a recent roadworthiness test (MoT in the UK) should require little or no mechanical work before a sale. The test, though, may have warned that certain work would be needed soon.

If your car has not been through such a test recently, you should consider whether it should to facilitate a sale. Cars with a lengthy roadworthiness test can be easier to sell, as it gives the buyer confidence, particularly for older models.

Drivers can quickly become aware of some mechanical faults, though, others can be less noticeable. Obvious signs include poor performance, or knocking, rattling or squeaking sounds if the brakes, fan belt, exhaust or other parts need replacing. Oil may be leaking, electric windows could be broken; the list is long.

Some problems can develop gradually, and may only come to light when you're checking over the car. Such faults can include a broken thermostat (which means your engine runs too cold), a faulty air mass meter (which leaves your car losing power) and worn wheel bearings.

Inevitably, you may have become accustomed to your car, so may be oblivious to some of its faults.

TOP TIP: Taking your car for a 'test drive' should help you understand how prospective buyers may view it. Try to imagine how they would feel while driving it. How does it sound? How does it smell? Perhaps you've got used to it pulling to one side, and you may now realise that it does this more than you thought. A car pulling to the side is dangerous, and may leave a viewer with nagging doubts over whether it has been involved in an accident. Often, however, this fault can be easily fixed – sometimes, by just properly inflating the tyres.

Mechanical problems should normally be sorted out first, to avoid wasting money improving the bodywork only to find that the engine is about to pack up, for example.

Unless you have the necessary expertise, the vast majority of electrical or mechanical problems, including oil leaks, should be fixed by professionals. Some minor oil seepages, which are quite common in older cars, are easy to clean using a degreasant or detergent.

Bodywork
Make an early assessment of what bodywork repairs, including dents, scratches and rust, are required. Give your car a quick wash, with a hose and brush attachment, a dry-off with a microfibre cloth and tea towel or chamois leather, and then inspect it.

TOP TIP: When using a hose/brush, hold the hose so it doesn't bang against, and potentially scratch, the bodywork.

Holding the hose to avoid scratching the paintwork.

The wrong way: the hosepipe could scratch the paintwork.

I recommend using hose/brushes which have a rubber casing and natural bristles (Lister produces such items). If you use a brush with a hard casing, be careful not to scratch your car.

TOP TIP: Tape around the casing edges and any metal on paintbrushes to avoid scratching paintwork.

Tape covering metal and edges which could scratch.

Brushes

While we're on the subject of brushes, I'll mention now that, ideally, you would have a range of paint, tooth, nail and scrubbing brushes, with soft, medium and harder bristles, for interior and exterior cleaning. Of course, you may not have such a collection, but the following are definitely needed, and should all be in good condition:

• A soft toothbrush for use on surfaces abutting paintwork or other materials which can scratch easily.
• A firm toothbrush for difficult-to-access and unlikely to scratch areas, and to clean wheels.
• A softish pure bristle paintbrush for the wet interior clean and hard-to-reach areas.
• An older, slightly stiffer pure bristle paintbrush for the brush-and-vac.

• A soft/medium nailbrush, preferably wooden-handled for good grip, and with acrylic bristles.
• A harder scrubbing brush to clean carpets, mats and tough plastics.
• A car-cleaning hose/brush.
• As a general rule, use softer brushes for surfaces that are likely to scratch easily, and harder ones for tougher materials/objects, such as carpets and foot pedals. New or newish toothbrushes, I find, work better, and are less likely to scratch than old, heavily-used items.
• Other brushes, such as a kitchen brush, can be useful to give you a longer reach.

TOP TIP: Always make sure all brushes are grit-free to avoid scratching.

When the car is clean, you then have to decide whether to:

• Take it to a bodywork shop for major repairs.
• Use a dentman to knock out dents, or perhaps have an expert remove scratches/chips.
• Do scratch or chip repairs yourself.

Repairs

Making decisions regarding bodywork repairs can be far from easy, and will be influenced by many factors, including whether you're selling or keeping your car, its age and condition, your finances, free time, and DIY skills. Skipping ahead to chapter five (paintwork repairs) may help you make up your mind. There you'll find explanations on how many superficial scratches can be easily repaired, how the impact of deeper ones can be significantly reduced, and how panels can be cleaned with colour-restorer.

Some bodywork damage may appear worse than it is, and you may be able to improve it considerably without major expenditure.

The prominence of paintwork flaws is also an important factor. For example, you'll probably be keener to get rid of a scratch on your bonnet or high up on the driver's door than one lower down on your car. You may be able to touch-in minor rust spots yourself.

If major scratches or rust could put off potential buyers, and you don't think you can make the necessary repairs yourself, it may be best to take the car to a professional at this stage; mending dents is best left to a specialist. A trusted local garage should be able to recommend a bodywork shop or dent/scratch repairmen. Dentmen, as well as scratch and chip repair experts, may come to your home, and be cheaper than a bodywork shop.

TOP TIP: If you've decided to have a scratch repaired professionally, you can always try doing it yourself now, in the knowledge that if it goes wrong you were always going to spend money getting it mended. You may surprise yourself by doing a satisfactory job.

It's best to repair scratches after the exterior wash, as you're bound to notice more as you clean the car.

Generally, cars up to around three years old should be prepared to as close to new condition as possible, so you should consider repairing most bodywork flaws – though try to work out whether any extra cost is likely to give you an equivalent or higher financial return. Sports cars and other rare models will normally also be expected to be in very good condition, no matter their age. Older family and other popular cars are generally not expected to be in such good condition, so a few scratches or stonechips, even a minor

indentation, are often not a problem. A good clean, colour-restoration and polish should considerably enhance their appearance.

Even vehicles in poor condition can be significantly improved, but if your car has widespread damage, it may be better to part-exchange it because it could be too costly to repair.

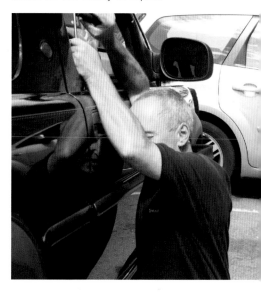

A dentman repairing a door.

It's essential during your check-over not to neglect basic maintenance tasks, such as correctly inflating tyres, and topping up fluid levels. These should be done, not only for your car's safety and performance, but also because if they are at low or incorrect levels they can give the impression of a vehicle that has not been looked after properly – as can failing to mend easy-to-fix faults, including broken bulbs and worn windscreen wipers. You should also find the car ownership documents and service history at this stage, and check they're up-to-date.

A full set of kit

From left to right downwards: Vacuum cleaner, with ear defenders (optional), bucket with washing up liquid, microfibre cloths, cleaning gloves, teatowel and chamois leather, thin paintbrush, bars of soap, camera, rubber brush and attachment, scrubbing brushes, nailbrushes, toothbrushes, trim finisher, old rubber glove, kitchen brushes, touch-up paint, colour-restorer, wet-and-dry paper, bucket with wet-and-dry paper in, margarine tub for soap, paintbrushes, cotton cloths, polish, protective glasses, wire brush and protective glove, acid-based cleaning agent, colour cutting compound, silver paint spray, jar with toothbrush for acid-based cleaner, tape to go around brushes to avoid scratching, paintbrushes for small gaps, hose with brush attachment around the kit (including a stop valve between the two sections), cup of tea.

two
Brush-and-vac

Kit
Vacuum cleaner (normal or wet-and-dry); one/two-inch (3-5cm) pure bristle, slightly stiff paintbrush (preferably used); a softer paintbrush; a thinner, longer, flat brush, for tight areas; scrubbing brush (preferably firm); rubber or latex gloves to remove dog hairs and fluff, particularly from velour seats and carpets (rub new gloves together to make them tacky); and hose section (optional).

Estimated time: One to three hours.
Goal: Basic inside clean.
Sale-booster factor: ✰✰ to ✰✰✰✰

Edges, edges, edges – areas are defined by edges
Dirty edges along seats, dashboard, doors, steering wheel, radio, and other areas reduce definition, sharpness and evenness, and leave the car appearing 'used,' and sometimes even shabby. Some can be easily cleaned, in as little as 20 seconds, while others are more difficult to access, and take far longer. It's always surprising how many edges there are in a car; some will be immediately obvious, but others are harder to spot. Look for joins in seats, stitching lines, gaps, sills, indented lines, areas where rubber seals meet metalwork, air vents, and even sunken numbers on a gear knob.

TOP TIP: If it's not flat, there's probably an edge of some sort.

How many edges on this door sill area?
Fewer than five? Count again!

This particular brush-and-vac job requires patience and hard work. The brushes are used to dislodge and push dust, dirt, sand, etc towards your vacuum cleaner's thin nozzle. This technique will mean that nooks and crannies are properly cleaned, as are vents and gaps, joins and corners.

I usually begin with the driver's area, as it's often the dirtiest, and proceed in the following order:

- Driver's door
- Dashboard
- Centre console, including vents, screens, radio, switches and gearstick
- Footwell – carpet and pedals
- The seat

Brush-and-vac along the window gap.

When you've finished the driver's area, work your way around the car, not forgetting the boot. This method can be adapted for people carriers (easier to clean with the rear seats removed), two-seater sports cars (no rear seats), and rear or mid-engined vehicles (boot and spare tyre at the front).

Front driver's side

The driver's seat may be the toughest to clean, but get it done and you should be filled with a glowing sense of achievement and a burst of enthusiasm to tackle the rest of the car. You may even find the work therapeutic.

Take out all the mats. Then, wind the driver's window right down so you can then clean the gap into which it has disappeared.

Starting at the windscreen end, use the tip of your paintbrush to work out dust and dirt towards the vacuum cleaner's nozzle, gradually moving along the window gap.

Next, clean the doorcard (the area below the window) using the same brush-and-vac technique along the handle, window controls, speaker grilles, door-pull and other edges. Flat areas may just require a quick vacuum without using a brush. Don't forget the door pockets!

Dashboard

Brush-and-vac the top of the dashboard (it might help if you sit in the car). Start in the bottom corner near the windscreen, and work your way across towards the passenger side, until you've cleaned just over halfway. Clean the dashboard between the steering wheel and the door, focusing on side vents and light switches, before cleaning the instrument area (includes the speedometer and other dials or information screens). Brushing-and-vaccing edges in this area is particularly important.

TOP TIP: Plastic dial or screen covers scratch easily, as can high gloss wood. If dusty, they can be lightly brushed with a good-condition, softish paintbrush, but they should not be touched by the vacuum nozzle.

Clean the top and sides of the steering column, including the ignition switch and the steering wheel itself. Some steering wheels can be adjusted for better access, but remember to put them back in your favoured position.

Clean the dial cover edges: don't touch them with the vacuum nozzle.

Tiny flecks of dead skin can be found around gearsticks.

Centre console

Clean the vertical section of the centre console, including the central vents, music systems, heater controls and other switches.

Brush-and-vac along the horizontal section of the centre console, which, in many cars, stretches back between the seats. The gearstick will probably need to be moved to fully clean the area at its base, which can be very dirty/dusty!

Footwell

Next, move the driver's seat right back (mind your fingers!) to clean the footwell.

TOP TIP: You can kneel on a padded surface, such as a mat, next to your car to make this job more comfortable. Vacuum and wet clean all the mats later.

Brushing-and-vaccing the gap between the seat and door can be tricky, but using a long thin brush will help. It's sometimes easier to clean this gap by getting the brush underneath the seat, to push dirt and dust upwards

A brush is great for removing dust from vents in the centre console.

Brushing dirt into the vacuum nozzle between the seat and door.

towards the vacuum nozzle, or vice versa. Clean the outside of the runners, on which the seat sits.

TOP TIP: Do not remove grease from the runners. Any grease that is transferred to the brush or vacuum cleaner nozzle should be removed at once so you don't spread it.

TOP TIP: Taping a small section of garden hose onto your vacuum nozzle can help with very narrow gaps.

Putting the vacuum nozzle under the seat to clean the gap.

Work down the doorside wall of the footwell, and around to the pedals, which will probably need scrubbing later. Cleaning below the pedals can be difficult, particularly if the accelerator is floor-mounted. This area is normally very dirty, so take the time to brush-and-vac it before doing the rest of the floor.

TOP TIP: A dry scrubbing brush will loosen ingrained dirt and sand on the floor. Remove all sand at this point, as it's harder to so during the wet clean. Vacuum the inside wall of the footwell, and then back between the seat and centre console. The thin brush will be handy for this tight gap.

The seat
Cleaning the seat is relatively easy. Start with the back, which normally just needs a vacuum.

Material seats, especially velour, gather more dust than leather does. Fluff, dog hairs and dust can be 'dragged' off the seats and carpets using a 'tacky' rubber or latex glove, and then vacuumed up.

Brush-and-vaccing the foot of the seat back where dirt lingers.

TOP TIP: Rub the glove in just one direction (as if you were stroking a cat) as this is the most effective way to use it.

The dirtiest area is nearly always the gap between the seat squab, the part you sit on, and the back. Material either side of hidden seams, stitching lines and creases on the squab should be gently stretched apart to brush-and-vac them. Some woven materials which have had heavy use can develop small 'bobbles.' They can be removed with a normal safety razor.

It can take more than half an hour to clean the driver's area, but if done properly the transformation can be remarkable. The other seats should be much quicker to clean.

Using a brush to clean seat stitching lines.

A thin layer of dust blurs the definition of the seat runner.

TOP TIP: To check the quality of your cleaning, vacuum one small area, eight to ten inches (20cm to 25cm) square, for five to ten minutes. You may be amazed by the difference.

Back seat (driver's side)
Move the driver's seat forward as far as possible. Wind down the window to brush-and-vac the gap, assuming the window has gone completely down (or along each side if it hasn't). Clean the doorcard, then do the rear of the driver's seat, using the same methods as for the front. Work your way around the footwell. Ashtrays and vents in the rear centre console may be dusty and dirty.

Position the brush and vacuum nozzle as far underneath the seat as you can to clean the floor, working backwards, towards the foot of the rear seat. Avoid grease on the runners. Check for grease on your tools before brushing-and-vaccing the rear seat, including the middle section. The far section will be done from the other side of the car. You can fold the back seats forward to clean underneath them.

Boot
The condition of boots can vary greatly. They can be in pristine condition or

Brush-and-vaccing sharpens the definition of the seat runner.

absolutely filthy. Some boots can be cleaned with just a brush-and-vac, starting high up and working your way down, but others will need a wet clean.

TOP TIP: Many boot carpets can be taken out, to dry or wet clean.

For hatchbacks, begin by vacuuming the parcel shelf. Then, take it

17

out, and do the top and rear of the back seats, followed by the turrets. Clean around the windows, before working down the sides.

TOP TIP: Don't press hard on parcel shelves with the vacuum cleaner, they can be easily marked.

For estate cars, remove the load-bay cover and clean the fixing points in which it sits. Load-bay covers often just need a wipe with a cloth, but may require a clean with a nailbrush and soap, and then a rinse.

TOP TIP: Fold the rear seats forward to clean their backs.

Patience, rather than brain power, is needed to clean boot carpets, which can require relentless vacuuming. Each small area can take time.

Use a rubber/latex glove to free dog hairs and other remnants caught in the fabric. Sand can be flicked up, using a scrubbing brush, into the vacuum nozzle.

Dog smells can be very hard to fully remove from cars. A thorough wet-and-dry clean of the interior will be needed, including areas which you would not expect to harbour pet odours. Dog hairs and debris can be found in the gap between the seats and the centre console, on levers, hinges and mechanisms, as well as under boot carpets and folding rear seats.

Clean the ledges on which the boot carpet sits, and also the spare wheel area. It is easier to clean the spare wheel well with the spare wheel removed.

TOP TIP: A dirty spare wheel area can give the impression of a lack of care. At this stage, check that your car has a full complement of spare wheel tools,

A filthy boot covered in dog hair.

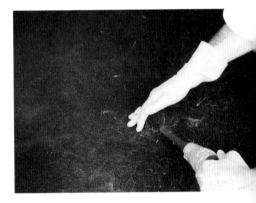

Sweeping out dog hair with a rubber glove.

The boot half brush-and-vacced.

The boot after a wet clean.

including a wheel brace, jack, and locking wheel nuts if required.

The boot lip, which includes the rubber seals and lock, is often very dirty, but should clean up easily. Remember to do the inside of the tailgate.

Don't forget the spare wheel cavity.

TOP TIP: Sitting inside the boot can make this task easier and more comfortable, rather than arching your neck at an awkward angle.

Second rear seat and passenger seat

You should by now have the knack of brush-and-vac, so cleaning the second rear seat, front passenger seat, and the second half of the dashboard should be quicker.

Cleaning the tailgate can be easier if you sit in the boot.

Brushing-and-vaccing a car can take several hours, depending on its size and condition. Once it's finished, though, your interior clean may be nearly done if your car was already in a good condition. However, for dirty cars, you may not be even halfway to achieving your goal.

three

Scrub and clean

Kit

• Wet-and-dry vacuum cleaner, bar of soap, microfibre cloth (to wipe clean-ish, easily scratched surfaces, including information screens, plastic dial covers and radios).
• A one to two inch (3cm to 5cm) pure bristle, softish paintbrush (to clean around the edges of easily scratched surfaces).
• A soft toothbrush, which should clean slightly better than the paintbrush, for grubby edges and gaps abutting other scratchable surfaces, including wood in the centre console. It's also used for intricate areas, such as switches.
• A firmer toothbrush for edges, corners and other tricky places on non-scratch materials.
• A medium (preferably wooden) nailbrush with synthetic bristles, and a scrubbing brush for grubbier, non-scratch areas, such as carpets and seats.
• Tea towel, towels, chamois leather, bucket, washing-up liquid, softish kitchen brush, margarine tub.

Estimated time: Two to three hours.
Goal: Stunning interior transformation.
Sale booster factor: ✰✰✰ to ✰✰✰✰✰.

A wet wash usually works wonders on cars, and the brush-and-vac should have you firmly on track to a gratifying interior make-over, but it's the scrub-and-clean that really makes the difference.

Caution! Before you start, remember the damage that water can do, particularly to electrics. This is why a wet-and-dry vacuum cleaner is vital for the full wet clean. On no account should an ordinary vacuum cleaner be used with water.

TOP TIP: To clean areas with electrical items, such as switches, electronic and audio systems, use a damp cloth and a toothbrush or paintbrush dipped in soapy water. Note, though, that the cloth should be damp, but not dripping, and that the water should be flicked off the brush so it's just wet, but also not dripping. You want the cloth and brush to be just wet enough to clean with, without allowing water to run down any surfaces that they touch, or into gaps. Dry off freshly cleaned areas as quickly as possible.

As a rule, you should vacuum dry all cleaned areas as soon as possible, to prevent water getting into hidden circuits, wires or connections, which may be under carpets or in other unexpected places.

The vacuum cleaner will suck out water from gaps, corners and other difficult-to-access areas. A tea towel can also be used to mop up spillages, but may not be as effective. **Note:** A conventional, dry-only vacuum is not suitable for this scrub-and-clean.

If you don't have a wet-and-dry vacuum, you can do a limited wet clean of the car's interior. This method is explained at the end of this chapter. You can also use upholstery foam cleaners, of course, though this can be an expensive option (I'm not a great fan of them).

Cleaning method

My method for wet cleaning is, generally, as follows:
- Wet, soap and clean an area with the cloth or one of the brushes, then swiftly vacuum off water, soap and dirt.

You will need to use your judgement, at times, to decide which brush is best for a particular task, while minimising the risk of causing scratches.
- Rinse seats and carpets with a wet and lightly wrung-out cloth. A slightly wet toothbrush or paintbrush can be used to rinse electrical and hard-to-access areas, making sure water doesn't drip or run down the surfaces. A second vacuum will be required as soon as possible to dry the area. If the area's still dirty, repeat the cleaning process above.
- Let the area dry naturally. The fan, air-conditioning (AC) and heating can also be used, and are essential in winter. Glass, chrome and high-gloss wood should be dried and polished, using a tea towel or chamois leather. Drying other surfaces with a tea towel can leave an uneven appearance.

Vacuuming soap and water from the doorcard.

Soap

With practice, you may master this cleaning technique, and be able to use just the right amount of soap and water to avoid an extra rinse and second vacuum. However, it's not worth cutting corners if it undermines your end result. You can use perfumed soaps, but those which have moisturizer may hamper your clean.

TOP TIP: Using too much soap wastes time. You need just enough to create a lather. If soap residue is left on a cleaned surface, rinse it by wetting it with a cloth or brush, before vacuum cleaning.

Be particularly careful not to use too much water. Wet fabric surface sufficiently so they are easy to clean, but don't allow too much water to seep into seats and carpets, as it will take longer to remove. As a guide, for fabric seats wring out the cloth two or three times, and then spread the water over it before scrubbing. Leather seats can be wiped with a wet cloth, prior to being scrubbed.

TOP TIP: Clean the seat last, or just before doing the floor, otherwise you'll get a wet bottom when you sit on it to do the dashboard, centre console and steering wheel.

Timing
The location and timing of a wet clean is important, as this will affect the ease with which you do it, how quickly your car dries out, and the final result.

TOP TIP: Always clean and paint your car in the shade, as direct sunlight tends to dry water and paint too quickly, resulting in a poor finish, including water stains. You can move the car into the sun after touching-in paintwork, or to help dry the interior. In summer, it's better to clean during a cooler part of the day – early morning, late afternoon or evening – because otherwise your car may dry too quickly, before dirt can be properly removed. On the other hand, in winter and other cold periods, you should be particularly aware of the need to dry your car as quickly as possible. Cleaning in the morning should allow the drying to start during the warmer middle part of the day.

TOP TIP: Don't clean (or try to dry) your car on rainy days. Check the weather forecast in advance.

Drying
In the heat of the summer your car should dry in direct sunlight within a few days. Leave the windows slightly open to allow the damp to escape, but without being open so much that the drying heat is lost. Obviously, think about security when leaving windows partially open.
Completely drying your car is crucial as water can result in unpleasant odours, cause fungal growths, and, in extreme cases, damage the car. Don't leave your wet car locked up for days, particularly in a garage. Fungal growth can normally be vacuumed off, followed by a soapy clean if necessary, but take health precautions, including trying not to breathe in spores.
However, you don't have to rely exclusively on mother nature to dry you car; you can also use the fan, heating and air-conditioning.
In cold and wet months, you'll definitely need the use of the heating and fan, and this will be significantly speeded up by putting on the A/C. Direct the fan towards the feet to dry the whole car, particularly the carpets.
Caution! DO NOT leave the engine running whilst the car is in an enclosed space (because of the risk of exhaust fume inhalation).

The clean
Collect your cleaning kit, fill a bucket with warm water, and take it all down to your car.

TOP TIP: Add a small amount of washing-up liquid to the water, to prevent water staining, especially in hard water areas. Don't add too much, though, because a frothy solution can

Wiping the top of the door frame.

Soaping up a nailbrush in a margarine tub helps keep the soap grit-free.

be difficult to remove. The water should be refreshed regularly, and cloths kept as clean as possible.

TOP TIP: Put the soap in an old margarine tub or similar container, with draining holes, to stop it picking up grit. Brushes can be placed in another container, or in the bucket, to keep clean.

So, where do you begin? There's no hard and fast rule, but this is the order in which I usually work:

Driver's door
Steering wheel
Dashboard
Centre console
Driver's footwell and pedals
Driver's seat
Rear driver's side seat area
Boot
Rear passenger side seat area
Front passenger side seat area
Windscreen and windows

Driver's side door

Wet the top of the driver's side door frame with a microfibre cloth, and wipe it down.

Felt or rubber may need a scrub with a soaped-up nailbrush (or a toothbrush for tight areas), before vacuuming dry, rinsing, and re-vacuuming. This is the basic cleaning method already mentioned, and so to avoid repeating 'vacuuming, rinsing, re-vacuuming' throughout this chapter, note that it should be done for most surfaces.

Dirt often streams from the lower rubber window seal.

Clean the inner and outer window seals. The top and side seals may need just a wipe-over with the cloth. The lower interior and exterior rubber seals, into which the window disappears, are often dirty, and you're likely to have to use the nailbrush to get them clean (use a toothbrush in the corners).

Fine-cleaning the door handle to improve its definition.

Scrubbing the doorcard with a nailbrush.

Clean-ish, flatter areas can often be cleaned with just a soapy microfibre cloth.

Use a soaped-up nailbrush for dirtier areas, and the stiffer toothbrush for edges, gaps and corners.

Cleaning the door switch (with a small amount of water, soap and a toothbrush).

Using a toothbrush to do the all-important detail cleaning.

Wet the doorcard from top to bottom, using the wrung-out microfibre cloth, taking care not to get switches or other electric items wetter than described in the Top Tip at the start of the chapter.

Continue to work your way down the door. Door handles can appear deceptively clean, so you may be surprised how much dirt can be scrubbed off with a nailbrush. A white film (of make-up or foundation) may also come off frequently-touched areas.

Drying a switch area after the clean.

As mentioned earlier, use only a damp cloth, toothbrush or paintbrush on switches and other electrics areas, and vacuum dry immediately.

Rubberised paint can peel off if scrubbed too hard.

TOP TIP: Check switches are properly attached, so they're not sucked into your vacuum.

Some door handles, steering wheels, switches and other parts are covered in rubberised paint, for a softer feel.

TOP TIP: Rubberised paint can be

damaged by hard scrubbing, so use a softer nailbrush, toothbrush or kitchen brush.

If rubberised paint is already damaged, through wear and tear, it's more likely to come off during a clean. If it does, you can improve the area's appearance by carefully picking off the pieces which are already peeling away. Beeswax furniture polish can be used

Using a kitchen brush makes cleaning door pockets easier.

to darken areas which have gone white after rubberized paint has flaked off. Door interiors which have been cleaned with silicon spray can look very shiny. A soapy scrub with a nailbrush should wash off this silicon layer, but it can take time to remove fully. Don't scrub too

Remember to clean the edges of the doorcard.

hard, and remember to do inside the door pockets.

TOP TIP: Use hot water when scrubbing out the remains of sticky sweets and the like. Some inks will not come off.

People often forget to clean the edges of the doorcard, next to locks and hinges. However, it's this type of detailed cleaning which really increases a car's appeal. Clean paintwork abutting the doorcard edges with the paintbrush, soft toothbrush and cloth.

Steering wheel

Because steering wheels are normally black, they're often grubbier than they might at first glance appear. Food residue, dead skin, grease and make-up may be smeared into the steering wheel.

Scrubbing around the steering wheel.

Wet the steering wheel with the cloth, and then scrub it with a nailbrush and toothbrush, taking care to limit the amount of water when cleaning switches, as already explained for electrics.

Don't forget the centre and back of the steering wheel.

TOP TIP: Hold the cloth behind the steering wheel, when scrubbing it with a brush, to stop the dashboard being sprayed.

Work methodically around the wheel with the nailbrush. If it's leather, carefully clean the stitching. Use the toothbrush for tight areas.

TOP TIP: Always scrub the steering wheel's back, to avoid having a smooth, clean front and a tacky back.

Clean the middle of the steering wheel and the column. If the steering wheel is adjustable, you can move it out and down for better access. Remember to put it back in place afterwards.

Dashboard

Start with the area between the steering wheel and the driver's door, cleaning each vent leaf individually with your toothbrush and a small amount of soap. The soapy toothbrush should, also, be used to clean other edges, including those on the vent panel, as well as switches and other controls.

TOP TIP: Cleaning vent leaves one by

Detailed cleaning to diminish the 'secondhand' look.

Dashboards can often be simply wiped clean with a damp cloth.

Wiping dial covers with a cloth to clean without scratching.

one may sound over-fussy, but it's this attention to detail that makes a car look its best.

Wipe over the top of the dashboard with a damp microfibre cloth (wetted in soapy water and wrung out). Dashboard edges which still appear dirty or are hard to reach can be cleaned with the toothbrush. They may need to be vacuumed and then left to dry. Dashboards which have been sprayed with silicon or other finishers may need several cleans with soapy water.

Scratches stand out on plastic dial covers and information panels in the instrument pod, so don't use a toothbrush or nailbrush to clean these surfaces. If they're dirty, clean them with a damp microfibre cloth, and buff them up with a dry tea towel.

Instrument pod gaps being cleaned with a softish paintbrush.

Clean edges, borders and partitions in the instrument pod with a softish paintbrush in good condition, taking extra care not to scratch. The vacuum nozzle can be used to suck up water around the edges, but it must not touch the plastic dial covers or instrument panels. Be very careful cleaning this area.

TOP TIP: Placing a dry, thin cloth over the vacuum nozzle will reduce the likelihood of scratching, but also the sucking power.

Centre console
Centre consoles come in all shapes and sizes, and contain lots of electrical components. They are normally quite grubby, and should be cleaned section by section, making sure you dry each one properly afterwards.

Air vents at the top of the centre console are best cleaned using a soapy toothbrush. A damp cloth, or a soft toothbrush which has been wetted

Removing grease, dead skin and dirt from the gearstick knob.

Cleaning radio screen edges on the centre console with a paintbrush.

Wet-and-dry vacuuming the radio avoiding scratching the screen.

and flicked to prevent water dripping, can be used on switches, including the emergency hazard lights, rear window demister, and other controls.

Clean information panels, audio systems, and other delicate surfaces with the damp cloth, or the paintbrush, and use a tea towel to buff up surfaces which should be shiny, including information panels, chrome switches and edging, and radio screens.

Work your way down the centre console, and onto the horizontal section. Use the same cleaning methods for this section, making sure you don't use too much water, to avoid it running down into switches.

The gearstick, handbrake, drink holders and centre armrest may need a thorough scrub. Moving the seat, backwards or forwards, will make it easier to clean the side of the console.

Footwell and pedals
Kneeling on a floor mat next to your car will give you a good position from which to scrub the pedals and footrest. Use the nailbrush, or scrubbing brush, and soap.

Scrubbing pedals (these can be filthy).

The pedals are likely to be very dirty, and are best cleaned along the line of any pattern, then vacuumed; they may not need a rinse. Also, clean the heel panel, the plastic area on which you rest your heel when driving.

Wet the microfibre cloth and wring it out several times on the carpet, spreading the water over it. If the carpet is very dirty you can clean it section by section. Rub soap directly onto

the carpet, before cleaning it with the nailbrush or scrubbing brush.

Make sure you do the corners, as well as carpet running up the footwell sides and centre console. Vacuum dry the carpet, pressing the nozzle firmly into it to extract water, and going over each area slowly. Repeat the process as many times as necessary. It may take up to four cleans to get a satisfactory result, especially with light-coloured carpets. Use slightly less water for repeat cleans, as the carpet will already be wet.

Wetting the back of the seat.

Dry vacuum the mats outside the car, pour water onto them, then soap them and scrub them. Don't forget to clean the stitching around the edges. The carpets can be rinsed with the hose, vacuumed, and then hung up to dry.

Scrubbing the soapy driver's carpet.

Scrubbing the back with a soapy nailbrush.

The seat

Refresh the bucket of water before cleaning the seat. Wet the headrest, the back (against which you lean) and sides using a cloth dipped in the water. The side nearest the door tends to be dirtier.

Soaping the seat squab.

If you are lucky, you can get away with just using the wet cloth to clean these areas. If they still look dirty, soap them up, and scrub them gently – to avoid damaging the fabric – with the nailbrush, before vacuuming, rinsing, and vacuuming again.

Use the same cleaning technique for the squab. It will almost certainly be

Vacuuming soap and dirt after the scrub.

dirtier, so you may need a second wash. Remember to do the sides, corners and adjustor, which can easily be missed.

Do not despair if cloth seats turn patchy as they dry out. Their appearance should improve significantly once completely dry.

Dirt-engrained leather seats.

TOP TIP: If dirt rises through seat material or carpets as they dry out, it can usually be wiped off using a damp microfibre cloth, once the fabrics are completely dry.

It's best not to let your seats stay wet for long, so the heating and A/C can be used to speed up the drying process. A towel can also be pressed onto the seat to absorb water. Sit on the towel if you need to drive the car.

Leather seats are often dirtier than they appear. The squab on the driver's seat, and other frequently-touched areas, tend to become shiny over time, while rear seats, and other less used areas, normally retain more of their original matt finish. A soapy scrub, using a nailbrush, is particularly good for cleaning leather; it should restore the matt texture to the seat.

Cleaning leather seats should give them a more even appearance.

Cleaning the door sill seal with a nailbrush.

Use a toothbrush for tight areas, and remember to clean the stitching.

TOP TIP: Cleaning the entire seat is important to get an even finish.

Be aware that dye sometimes comes off leather. It may look like dirt, especially if it's a grey or black

If leather seats look patchy, this can mean that they are still dirty, so you may want to repeat the cleaning process.

Wiping the inside of the B-pillar.

A grubby seat spoils the car's appearance ...

seat. If this happens, scrub the whole area briefly, and very lightly, with your nailbrush, before vacuuming it, giving it a quick rinse, and re-vacuuming.

Leather seats can take longer to clean than cloth seats. Occasionally, cleaning leather seats can result in white patches,

... but is transformed after a wet clean.

even after rinsing away all the soap. However, a matt leather conditioner should restore their appearance.

Finish off the driver's seat area by cleaning the seatbelts, if necessary, with a cloth, as well as the B-pillar, which is between the front and rear door.

The internal door sill, including the rubber seal, can be washed using the nailbrush.

Now, stand back and you should be able to bask in the glory of one clean seat.

Then, it's time to get on with cleaning the rest of the car, using the same methods.

Rear driver's side
Move the driver's seat forward as far as possible, to create space to clean the area behind it. Start with the doorcard on the driver's side rear door. The rear of the driver's seat may just need wiping down with a cloth.

Scrubbing clean the seat runner cover.

Clean the runners on which the seat sits, and their covers, using a scrubbing, kitchen or toothbrush. Remember to avoid any greasy areas.

Wash the carpet, using the same technique used to clean the driver's footwell. Scrub vents and other parts of

Sprucing up the rear console vents.

with an appropriate brush or cloth, can be awkward. This task can be done by having the tailgate open, and getting underneath it, but you may get wet – or by sitting in the boot, which may be more comfortable.

Some boot carpets are removable, and so can be cleaned outside and hung up to dry – it's best to do this if they are very dirty. To clean carpeted areas inside the boot, start with the sides – soap them up, scrub them, then move down to clean the main carpet. The ledges on which the carpet sits may also need cleaning.

the centre console, which may extend between the front seats into the rear, with the nailbrush and toothbrush.

The driver's side rear seat and the middle section of the rear seats should be cleaned using the same methods used for the driver's seat. Rear seats in people carriers can be removed to aid cleaning and allow access to the floor.

The boot
Loose dirt, dog hair and other debris should already have been vacuumed out of the boot. Scrubbing the carpet thoroughly, with the nailbrush or scrubbing brush, should improve it further, and get rid of most smells. Very dirty boot carpets may require cleaning and vacuuming as many as four times. Slightly less water and soap can be used for repeat cleans. It's not necessary to rinse the carpet between each scrub-and-vacuum, but give it a rinse-and-vacuum at the end.

However, before doing the carpet, clean around the windows with a toothbrush. Load-bay covers can be wiped over with a cloth, or cleaned with the nailbrush, preferably outside the vehicle. The backs of the rear seats should only rarely need cleaning.

Cleaning the inside of the tailgate,

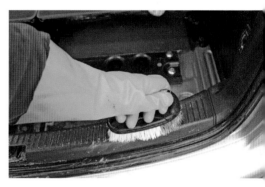

Scrubbing the internal plastic boot sill.

Normally, the spare wheel area just needs vacuuming, which should already have been done, but if it's particularly filthy, take it out and wash this cavity and the wheel itself.

After cleaning the boot, check that no water has seeped into the spare wheel well. It could linger there and cause bad smells and corrosion.

A detailed scrubbing of the plastic sill, including the rubber seal, should enhance the boot's overall appearance.

Clean the remaining seats and doors, the second half of the dashboard, and the outside of the glove box, using the skills you used for the driver's area.

Windscreen and windows

For the final act, clean the inside of the windscreen and windows, having first removed any stickers which could hinder a sale.

TOP TIP: Sticker adhesive residue should come off using polish, white spirit, or glue remover.

Starting on the driver's side, clean just over half of the windscreen using a microfibre cloth dipped in fresh water. Remember to put a dash of washing-up liquid in the water, and to work the cloth into the screen's corners and edges. Wipe off water and dirt from this section, with the rinsed and wrung-out cloth, then buff up with a tea towel. The rubber around the windscreen may need cleaning with a soapy toothbrush.
Clean the rear view mirror with the cloth, and then the driver's side front window, before working your way around the car, finishing with the second half of the windscreen.

TOP TIP: Lower windows slightly so you can clean the top, otherwise you'll see a marked line a few centimetres (half an inch or so) down the glass when they're next wound down. Wind up the windows to clean the bottom few centimetres.

With your car's windows and interior sparkling, you can congratulate yourself on a job well done!
Crucially, though, you now must make sure that the car dries completely. Moving it into a sunny spot, or using the A/C, heating and the fan will help, but it may be several days before it's fully dry.

TOP TIP: Don't put the mats back in until the carpet is absolutely dry.

Buffing up windows with a tea towel

may have left dust in the car. This can be removed with a swift brush-and-vac.

Limited wet clean

A very thorough brush-and-vac is vital for the limited wet clean. Folded towels, preferably old, and a microfibre cloth will substitute for the wet-and-dry vacuum, in removing water and dirt from carpets and seats.

TOP TIP: You can stand, where possible, sit or press down on the towels to soak up water.

Note, though, that towels and the wrung-out microfibre cloth, which is also used for drying other areas, will not be as effective as a wet-and-dry vacuum. Therefore, use less water when cleaning the car, and make sure it's allowed to dry thoroughly afterwards – using the heating, A/C and fan – especially in cold and wet periods. Obviously, it's far better to do this clean in dry weather.
Clean switches and other electrical areas with a damp microfibre cloth dipped in soapy water. Make sure water doesn't run down any surfaces and/ or into gaps. Try to get into every nook and cranny. These areas can be dried with a rinsed-clean and completely wrung-out microfibre cloth. The same method is used for the centre console and dashboard. Use a toothbrush or paintbrush dipped in soapy water for particularly grubby areas, gaps and edges, where there are no electrics, before wiping them with a wrung-out microfibre cloth.
Clean carpets and seats with the microfibre cloth – dipped in soapy water and then wrung out. Areas should be repeatedly wiped over with the cloth, which should be regularly rinsed in a bucket of clean water. The surfaces should be only slightly wet, to rub clean, rather than allowing water to seep in.

Particularly dirty seats and carpets
If the carpets and seats are very dirty, you can wet and scrub them as per the standard wet-clean, though using less water, but you may have to pull up the carpet to dry underneath it with a towel. I don't advise this wetter clean on carpets unless you're sure you know how to take up the carpet, and that there are no electronics located under it.

If you do this fuller clean, once you have scrubbed the carpet or seat, wipe it off, with a fully wrung-out microfibre cloth, to remove dirt and water. Rinse the cloth, and repeat the clean until you've removed the worst of the dirt. Next, clean the cloth in a fresh bucket of water, wring it out, and rinse off the area again, possibly several times. This may clean it sufficiently, but it may need more scrubbing and rinsing. Push the cloth as far as possible into the carpet or seat to remove water and dirt. Leather seats and non-electric areas, including sills and other non-scratchable plastics, can be wetted, scrubbed with a soaped-up nailbrush or toothbrush, and then wiped off with the wrung-out microfibre cloth.

Areas which can scratch easily should be cleaned with the damp microfibre cloth and a tea towel.

All areas must then be made bone-dry, using the towels, heating, fan and A/C.

four
The big wash

This chapter explains how to dramatically transform your car's wheels, and clean exterior paintwork and semi-interior areas, including doorshuts and the engine compartment.

Kit
Bar of soap, nailbrush, hose, hose nozzle, hose/brush attachment for cleaning cars, bucket, soft and firmer toothbrushes, kitchen brush,

Dirty wheels will spoil the car's appearance.

Only the wheels have been cleaned, but already this car looks better.

paintbrush, scrubbing brush, microfibre cloths, tea towel or chamois leather, washing-up liquid. Wheel cleaning agent, towel, wire brush, protective gloves, bolt paint, black trim finisher, waterblade, degreasant, colour-restorer, chrome and shiny metal polish finishers (optional).

Estimated time: Two to six hours.
Goal: Rejuvenate your car's exterior.
Sale-booster factor: ✰✰✰ to ✰✰✰✰

Washing the outside of a car is easy if you want a basic clean. However, if you're after a dazzling, eye-catching, as-close-to-original finish as possible, you need skills, hard work and a relentless focus on detail.

TOP TIP: In my view, wheels are visually the most important exterior part of a car. That may surprise you, and indeed most people do regard the paintwork as the most important. However, smart wheels in all their sharply-defined metallic glory, will immediately grab a viewer's eye.

In summer, it's easier to wash cars in the morning or late-afternoon/early evening rather than during the midday heat.

I advise cleaning a car in the following order:

1. Soft tops
2. Wheels
3. Hosing down the car's lower part
4. Doorshuts, under the bonnet and bootshut
5. The clean itself:
   a. Roof
   b. Windscreen
   c. Bonnet, grille, lights, bumper and valance
   d. Sides and back
6. Drying

Soft tops
If you don't have a soft top, I would still strongly recommend reading this section because it includes useful tips, particularly on the importance of detailed cleaning and avoiding scratching, which applies to all cars. Soft tops are often dirtier than many people realise. If you first cleaned

A greenish moss-like residue builds up in gaps and gulleys.

A cleaned section of a sunroof edge.

the body of the car, you may have to re-wash it after dirt has streamed down from the soft top.

Cars kept outside will also almost certainly have some green, mossy-like dirt on them, often on and around soft tops, around sunroofs, at the bottoms of windows, and around badges. Removing it significantly improves a car's definition.

Most soft tops should be scrubbed clean with soap and a fairly stiff nailbrush or medium scrubbing brush. This scrubbing method should also remove that green dirt, but it's not suitable for old soft tops which may have become brittle.

It's very important to clean the whole of the soft top, including the edges. Use a toothbrush to clean the very edge where it meets the body of the car.

Soft tops on new cars, or those which have largely escaped being weather-beaten, may need just a clean with the hose/brush.

As a general rule, never use a toothbrush, nailbrush, scrubbing brush or kitchen brush on paintwork, as they can scratch.

Cleaning the very edge of a soft top with a toothbrush.

A soft toothbrush can be used, with caution, where paintwork butts up to other surfaces, including around badges, bumper strips, rubbing strips, soft tops, and sunroofs.

TOP TIP: The toothbrush bristles should, as far as possible, only contact the non-paintwork surface.

The toothbrush can also be used in the gaps and tight corners in some semi-concealed paintwork areas, such as the bootshut, rear numberplate recess, and around door hinges.

The paintbrush is also suitable for these areas, particularly for flatter paintwork.

Check regularly for new scratches, and, if your brush is causing them, use a softer brush. Fortunately, scratches from brushes tend to be minor, and can normally be successfully polished out with colour-restorer.

To begin, wet the soft top using a hose or water from a bucket (with a dash of washing-up liquid in). In the winter, using a bucket of warm water will stop your hands getting too cold. A hose provides a good water supply for rinsing.

Scrubbing a largish section of a soft top in autumn.

TOP TIP: Wearing thin, woolly gloves, under washing-up gloves, in very cold weather keeps your hands warm.

Once the soft top is wet, rub soap over one area and then scrub it, using your nailbrush or scrubbing brush; first in the direction of the stitching, and then across it.

TOP TIP: Don't use a scrubbing, nail or toothbrush to clean plastic rear screens on soft tops, as you risk scratching them.

If it's a cold day, you can scrub the whole roof in one go, without it drying out. However, on a hot summer's day, do it in small sections.

Rinse
Fully rinse each section, to avoid leaving soap residue. While rinsing, go over the area again with the scrubbing brush, to get out all soap, and to wash any remaining dirty patches.

Rinsing off a soaped soft top.

The small section of material, situated underneath the rear screen is often very dirty, and may need a good scrubbing. Lightly clean the outside of the screen later, using the hose/brush and a microfibre cloth.

It's hard to see how clean soft tops are when they're wet, and many will need several washes to return them to a good condition, so let them dry out between washes. You can use your wet-and-dry vacuum to dry them more quickly.

Wheels

Rarely will people exclaim: "Wow, what clean wheels!" However, properly cleaned wheels make an immediate good impression.

Initially, try to clean wheels or wheel trims, not the tyres at this stage, using a bucket of water, a toothbrush or kitchen brush, and soap. If this is all that's needed, you'll be spared the harder work of using a wheel-cleaning fluid.

Choose a wheel – front ones tend to be dirtier – and wet it with a hose, or by splashing it with water from your bucket. Obviously, it's best not to do this straight after driving the car, as the brakes and wheels could still be hot. Scrub the wheel, inch-by-inch, with a wet and soaped-up toothbrush.

Start with the edge between the wheel and tyre, working your way around the wheel to get a well-defined edge.

Cleaning with a toothbrush to get a sharply-defined edge.

Wheel edges are often 'kerbed,' and may have gone black or dull. Acid-based, wheel-cleaning fluid should smarten them up.

Once you've cleaned the outside of the wheel, work your way towards the centre.

TOP TIP: Divide your wheel into sections to clean, as it will get dirty, and you may struggle to remember which bits you've done.

Having done a few sections, you may notice that the wheel is not scrubbing up as well as you would like, so you may have to use wheel-cleaning fluid. If the wheel is smartening up to your satisfaction, complete the other sections, and check for any missed areas.

TOP TIP: Missed areas should be easy to spot if you move your car forward by around half a wheel turn.

Wheel-cleaning fluids

Motoring shops, valeter supply merchants and other stores sell a selection of wheel-cleaning fluids. Some are acid-based, while others use different technologies, compounds and formulas, including surfactants. I make up my own acid-based cleaner, diluting it with water for different jobs, but for the vast majority of people it's probably simpler to buy a wheel-cleaning product.

Acid-based cleaners are particularly effective at cleaning wheels, but new products are always being developed. Choosing a suitable product is vital, so check the label; I wouldn't use acid-based cleaners on magnesium alloy and chrome spoke wheels.

TOP TIP: Some cleaning agents may dull wheel surfaces slightly, but they can be brightened up again with the application of colour-restorer and polish.

Caution! Be very careful when using wheel-cleaning fluids, especially acid-based ones. Follow the instructions and warnings carefully! Always wear gloves, protective glasses, protective clothing, including a long-sleeved-shirt and trousers. I brush, rather than spray, on the cleaning agent, rinse off splashes on skin quickly, and keep it out of reach of children and pets. In addition, I swiftly rinse off surfaces on which the acid-based agent has been; don't leave the brush standing in the cleaner, and properly dispose of any leftovers.

You may need to take different precautions for other wheel-cleaning products, and use them in different ways, so always check the instructions. Some are available in the form of sprays, whilst others are brushed on.

TOP TIP: I don't advise using acid-based agents for regular wheel cleaning: I use it only when selling the car or doing a major revamp.

To follow my method, pour a small amount of acid-based solution into a glass jar. Diluting it with water will make it less powerful, but gentler on your wheels. It's best to start with a weak solution and add more cleaner if needed. Most off-the-shelf wheel cleaners should be ready-to-use.

Wet the wheel, and then scrub it with a toothbrush that's been dipped in the cleaning agent, before quickly rinsing the area with the hose/brush.

Follow the steps you took previously when using the toothbrush and soap; starting on the edge and moving inward.

Caution! Brushes used with wheel cleaner have very limited uses afterwards, and certainly none in the kitchen or bathroom!

The harder the car's been driven, the more difficult the wheels are to clean. Some can need three or four washes, while others can be done in one go. Always rinse wheels and tyres properly.

The insides of wheels may also need cleaning on some models, such as high-spec sports cars, because they're highly visible. The inside is the area visible from the outside, not the back of the wheel.

If you decide to clean the inside, try a soapy wash first. A kitchen brush can be useful, as it has a longer handle.

Cleaning the inside of the wheel with a toothbrush.

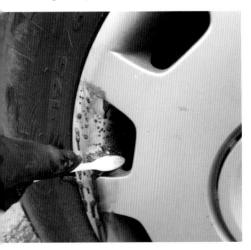

Cleaning a wheel trim with a toothbrush and acid-based cleaner.

However, you'll probably also have to use wheel-cleaning fluid to remove any black grime (mainly brake dust).

If so, wet and scrub the inside with a brush, dipped in cleaning agent, taking care not to splash yourself, then thoroughly rinse all cleaned areas and the tyre. Repeat if necessary, but remember, acid-agent can dull wheels.

Caution! Don't clean brake pads and discs, but you can clean brake calipers. If you're unsure about brake parts, don't clean any of them.

Wheels may have little black dots, which are encrusted dust spots. They can be difficult to remove, but may come off with repeated use of cleaning agent and a toothbrush, followed by a rinse.

Sports cars and some other models often have highly-visible, coloured brake calipers. These can normally be washed

Cleaning a brake caliper with a toothbrush.

with a soapy clean, but the use of cleaning agent may be required (quickly wash it off the caliper and the brush you used).

If the wheels are in a terrible state they can be refurbished, but this can be costly, so calculate whether it's worth it.

Wheel bolts

Wheel bolts usually can't be seen, and so don't need cleaning. Sports models, however, often have visible wheel bolts, and these may need to be cleaned.

It's easiest to clean them once they've been removed from the wheel, so take all of them out, bar one per wheel. **Caution!** Don't drive your car until all wheel bolts have been replaced! You don't need to jack up the car because you're not taking off the wheels.

Once the bolts are out, use an acid-based wheel-cleaning agent and a toothbrush to remove rust and dirt.

If this doesn't do the job, try rubbing them down with a wire brush; avoiding the bolt threads. Finally, spray them with two or three fine coats of original colour paint, normally silver.

TOP TIP: Painted bolts cure well in direct sunlight.

Wearing gloves when using a wire brush will protect your hands. The bolt holes, which should be more accessible, can also be cleaned.

TOP TIP: Make sure the painted bolts

Wire brushing a bolt.

are completely dry before carefully screwing them back in – you could break the paint with the wheel brace.

After they're back in, remove the remaining bolt to clean/repaint it.

Tyres
While the paint on the wheel bolts is drying, you can get on and clean the tyres' outer sidewalls. The best way to do this is to spray them with a pressure washer, from a distance of at least 20cm. You hardly ever need to clean the tyre tread.

Pressure-washing a tyre sidewall.

Dirty sills, wheels and wheelarches spoil the car's appearance.

This car has been cleaned top to bottom.

TOP TIP: When tyres are wet, it's difficult to distinguish the cleaned areas from those still to be done, so pressure-wash methodically, and slowly.

If you don't have a pressure washer, use the hose/brush, as well as a scrubbing or nailbrush, and soap. Wet the tyre and scrub it, starting on one small area, and going around it clockwise or anti-clockwise. Use the hose/brush to remove soap and dirt.

Dirty, faded and indistinct plastic trim.

TOP TIP: It's easier to clean tyres by following the pattern on the outside sidewall of the tyre – these can include fine grooves, tyre size, make, etc.

Black trim finish can be applied at the end of the outside clean, to give faded tyre walls a more original look; but don't put it on the tyre tread.

Caution! To avoid damaging the tyres, use a light-to-medium duty pressure washer (110bar or less), keep the washer jet nozzle at least 20cm from the tyre surface, always use a fan nozzle to clean tyres, rather than a circular nozzle, avoid prolonged exposure to a specific area of the tyre, and don't aim the water jet directly at the join between the tyre and the wheel rim.

Hose down
Before cleaning the body of the car, pressure wash or hose down the wheelarches and the lower part of the vehicle if it's dirty; this reduces the risk of dirt and grit scratching paintwork as you clean it. Make sure that you've washed right down to the bottom of the sill.

TOP TIP: Cleaning to the bottoms of the sills, in the wheelarches, and into other recesses ensures a car exudes cleanliness upwards and outwards.

Remember to wash the bumpers, rubbing strips, and other trim. Clean unpainted, rough-finished plastic with a pressure washer, or with the hose/brush and nailbrush, and soap; use your soft toothbrush for edges abutting paintwork.

Sharply-defined, even and clean plastic trim.

Clean painted bumpers later, during the main wash, using a microfibre cloth.

TOP TIP: You can use your fingernails, provided they're not too short or too long, through the cloth, to get bumper and trim edges looking sharp.

Doorshuts
After this initial washdown, it's time to turn to the 'semi-exterior' areas. Sides and sill areas of doorshuts and the sides and bottoms of doors should be cleaned with your hose/brush. Use a soapy paintbrush or toothbrush for intricate areas, such as locks. You may

be overlapping slightly here with the interior wet clean.

Paintwork at the tops of doorshuts and doors can be wiped clean with a wet microfibre cloth. The hose/brush, with a very low water flow, can also be used, but be careful not to get water inside your car.

Lay a towel on the seat to keep it dry, and quickly dry off any water which goes inside with a tea towel or the wet-and-dry vacuum, particularly on electric areas.

TOP TIP: To temporarily slow or stop water flow, put a kink in the hosepipe (so you don't have to walk back to the tap). Alternatively, you can fit a stop valve on the end of the hose, so water only flows once an attachment is connected. Both methods save water.

Some cars have felt in the doorshuts and on doors, and this should be cleaned with a cloth, nailbrush or toothbrush, and soap, before rinsing with the hose/brush or wet-and-dry vacuuming. Dirt can also build up between rubber seals and paintwork, or in double-formed rubber seals, particularly on doorshut sills and gulleys. Wet these areas, and scrub them with the nailbrush or toothbrush.

Detailed cleaning on a doorshut (using a soft toothbrush).

Washing a doorshut.

Dirt in a doorshut top gulley.

45

A clean gives the gulley a sharp finish.

When doing rubber seals on the tops of doorshuts, hold a cloth underneath to catch falling water and dirt. These areas can then be wet-and-dry vacuumed, or rinsed off with the hose/brush. Remember to dry off any wet interior areas.

Using a cloth to catch dirt and water when cleaning a doorshut.

Paintwork on cleaned sills may show scratches, often caused by the seatbelt buckle. You may be able to repair some of them yourself.

Avoid grease on door hinges and other parts, as it will clog up your brush. Getting grease off components is very difficult, and you normally have to re-apply it.

Engine

Before cleaning the engine compartment, make sure the engine has properly cooled. **Caution!** Don't burn your hand when checking. Spraying a hot engine with water, particularly the exhaust manifold, can damage it.

TOP TIP: Turn on the engine after cleaning it, to help the drying process, particularly in cold weather.

The engine compartment doesn't have to be as sparkling clean as the rest of the paintwork, but it can often be tidied up with a limited wash with your hose/brush and a cloth.

Most electrical parts on modern cars are sealed, but it's always advisable to avoid getting them too wet. Try not to spray too much water around, as it can cause problems; for example, with sparkplugs and leads.

Caution! Older cars may have broken/damaged/badly fitting seals around electrics, so this technique may not be suitable for them.

TOP TIP: Don't use a pressure washer or steam cleaner in the engine compartment.

Pick out leaves and other debris from the engine compartment's rear corners, near the windscreen. These areas can be hosed out, with the brush attachment off. Use a toothbrush and a paintbrush to clean into corners.

Put the brush attachment back on and set the water to low flow to wash the area below the windscreen, where the wipers are attached. It's easiest to do this, standing by the driver's side front wheel.

Clean this area, as far as you can comfortably reach across the car, using the paintbrush and toothbrush if needed. Avoid banging the hose against the side of the car.

Wash the section where the wing is bolted to the driver's side of the compartment. Clean the strut tops, engine cover, coolant container, windscreen washer bottle, and other non-electrical parts, including plastic covers and hoses.

Slow flow of water to clean the side of the engine compartment.

Wash the slam panel, which includes the top of the lights and centre grille, before doing the opposite side of the compartment and the second half of the area below the windscreen.

Cleaning the slam panel.

TOP TIP: Cleaning the side edges of the bonnet with the hose/brush or a toothbrush is a good finishing touch.

Fine-cleaning the side of the bonnet for a sharp finish.

Oily engine covers can be cleaned with a degreasant (liquid laundry detergent can also work).

Cleaning the underneath of the bonnet isn't essential, but for most cars you would ideally do it. Take care, though, as you're more likely to spray water around the engine compartment, increasing the possibility of damaging electrical components.

Wet the underneath of the bonnet with the hose, and then scrub it with the soaped-up hose/brush, with the water off. Turn the water back on, to hose/brush down the bonnet's underneath and other areas which have become dirty, trying not to get them too wet.

Bootshut
The bootshut (I'll also call tailgate shuts bootshuts, for simplicity's sake) is a tricky area. To begin, open the boot (on saloon cars) or tailgate (on hatchbacks and estates), and clean the strip of horizontal paintwork, above the top rubber seal, where the boot/tailgate hinges are usually located.

Cleaning the bootshut with a soft paintbrush.

Put your hose above the bootshut, so water slowly flows down onto it, and wash away dirt with a paintbrush or toothbrush.

An eye-catchingly clean bootshut.

Dirt can build up in bootshuts.

The vertical sides of the bootshut can be washed with the hose/brush and paintbrush.

Remember to clean the sides and bottom of the boot/tailgate with a hose/brush, and paintbrush and/or toothbrush if necessary, trying not to get water inside the car.

Cleaning the vertical side of a bootshut.

TOP TIP: Partially opening the boot/ tailgate can limit the amount of water going into the car.

Cleaning paintwork on the underside of a partially-open boot.

The wash
As already mentioned, the wash should be done in the shade, to avoid getting white staining marks on paintwork from water, particularly hard water, drying too quickly.

TOP TIP: Soap sticks/tablets can be inserted in some brush/attachments to reduce the risk of staining.

The roof
Wash the front of the roof with the hose/brush, starting in the middle and working towards the driver's door. To avoid missing patches, imagine that you're painting the roof a different colour.

For 4x4s, or other tall cars, you might need to stand on a chair/step ladder, but be careful not to crash it into the car.

Gradually, work your way down the roof towards the boot. Clean the second half of the roof from the other side.

TOP TIP: The tips of the bristles on the

Holding the hose to avoid scratching when cleaning the roof.

hose/brush are better at removing dirt than the sides.

Clean the felt and rubber edges around sunroofs with a toothbrush, but beware of scratching the paintwork.

Other detailing on the roof, including gulleys, can be cleaned with the hose/brush or a paintbrush. Remove stubborn marks by repeating the cleaning process, rather than using excessive force.

Toothbrush bristles are mainly on the sunroof when cleaning an edge.

TOP TIP: Dirt on sponges can scratch, so I don't advise using them.

Roof racks and rails

Dirt often becomes ingrained along roof rails, or around roof rack bolts and supports, but should come off with the toothbrush or paintbrush.

TOP TIP: Many cars look untidy with a roof rack. You can take it off and sell it separately, offer it as an extra, or throw it in 'for free' to sweeten the deal.

Windscreen

Clean the edge between the roof and windscreen with a toothbrush.

Wash A-pillars (between the windscreen and the window sections of the front doors) with the hose/brush,

Cleaning the gap between the roof and windscreen.

using the toothbrush for where they meet the glass.

Wash the windscreen, using the hose/brush, with the wipers up and from the top down.

TOP TIP: Microfibre cloths are good for removing dead flies.

Gently clean the windscreen wiper arms with the hose/brush, using the toothbrush for around the base of the wiper arms and along the bottom of the windscreen.

Bonnet

Wash the bonnet with the hose/brush, starting at the top near the windscreen. Clean it in sections, working down towards the front of the car.

TOP TIP: Laying a hot wet cloth on stubborn bird droppings for ten minutes should soften them, making them easier to remove.

Next, clean the front of the car, including the grille, lights and numberplate.

This area is often dirty, and has loads of edges, indentations and different surface finishes. Clean it with a soapy toothbrush and microfibre cloth, dipped in water with washing-up liquid, before rinsing it with the hose/brush.

Water stains around the edges of metal badges and chrome grilles can

Smartening up around the lights.

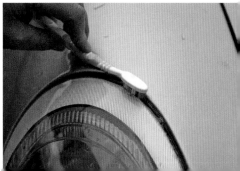

be removed with a toothbrush and a suitable acid-based cleaning agent. It can also be used on rust staining around numberplate screws. Swiftly rinse any areas cleaned with the agent and the toothbrush because this is a highly visible part of your car.

Clean the bumper's painted section using a microfibre cloth if needed, followed by the very bottom section –

Wheelarches and lower sills stand out if dirty.

Cleaning the front vents with a toothbrush.

the front valance – where fog lights are generally situated. Use the toothbrush, cloth and hose/brush.

The sides

Clean the sides one section at a time. I tend to start with a wing, washing it with the hose/brush, including the paintwork on the inside edge of the wheelarch and visible parts of plastic wheelarch liners.

Before cleaning the paintwork again, check that you haven't picked up dirt on the brush.

TOP TIP: A dirty brush can be cleaned by using it to wash the side of a tyre until the water runs clean.

Next, wash the front door section, including the window, with the hose/brush, starting from the top. Use the toothbrush around windows, mirrors, handles, locks and rubber mouldings.

Sills can require repeated cleaning with the hose/brush; applying a dash of washing-up liquid on a microfibre cloth, can help.

Repeat the wash for the rear door section and the rear wing.

You can clean the rear of the fuel flap and around the fuel cap with an appropriate brush, but don't open the cap itself.

Rear

The rear can be very dirty, and you'll probably need to use the toothbrush,

Cleaning inside the fuel filler flap, with the cap firmly on.

paintbrush and hose/brush. Areas to focus on include the gap at the bottom of the rear windscreen on tailgated cars, badges, and the rear numberplate recess.

TOP TIP: Detailed cleaning of rear badges is vital to give many cars that nearly-new look. You may need to use an acid-based cleaning agent and toothbrush.

Pull back the windscreen wiper to wash it. Clean the rear plastic screen on soft tops with the hose/brush and a clean microfibre cloth, checking that neither is scratching it. Wring out the cloth to dry the screen, but don't press too hard as it's easily scratched.

Dirt often accumulates in the numberplate area and in other rear recesses, and where lights may be situated. Clean these areas with the hose/brush and a paintbrush.

Wash the top of the bumper (should be easy), and then the other rear areas, including the lights, focusing on the edges.

Drying
Dry the entire car, apart from the tyres, using a thoroughly cleaned microfibre cloth; waterblades can also be used. Dry off any remaining water with a cotton tea towel or a slightly damp chamois leather. Dry the underneath of the bonnet last using just a microfibre cloth.

Brown exhaust stains sometimes form on the rears of cars. These can be polished off using a colour-restorer, as explained later.

Chrome and bright metal exhaust pipe finishers can be smartened up, when cool, with an acid-based cleaning agent, taking all the precautions already mentioned. Other metal or chrome cleaners, colour-restorers, and metal polishes can also be used. This task can require a lot of work.

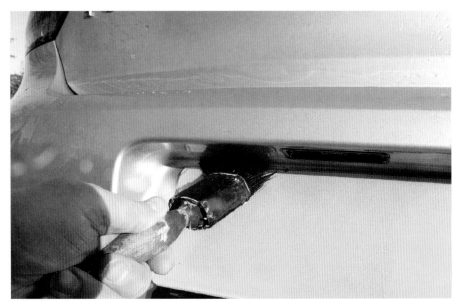

Cleaning right into the rear numberplate recess with a paintbrush.

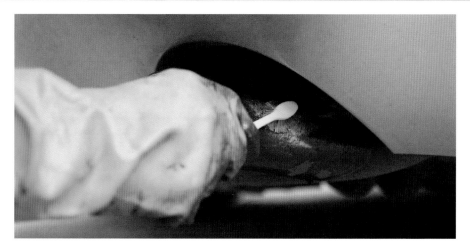

Cleaning an exhaust pipe finisher with acid-based agent.

Polishing an exhaust pipe finisher with metal polish.

TOP TIP: Always clean and colour-restore exhaust finishers last, as your cloth and brushes are likely to get dirty.

five

Repair and shine

Kit
Car polish, colour-restorer, very fine wet-and-dry paper, smooth rubbing block, touch-up paint, cotton cloths, microfibre cloth, paintbrush, toothbrushes (used), clean tea towel, clean rag.

Estimated time: One to many hours.
Goal: Return to as close to new appearance as possible.
Sale-booster factor: ☆ to ☆☆☆☆.

Pride and a deep sense of satisfaction should, hopefully, now be negating any tiredness and aches and pains as you inspect your thoroughly clean car. In many cases, though, you'll be able to make your paintwork radiate even more depth, colour and shine. However, you may find that cleaning has revealed more scratches. Given that significant bodywork repairs should already have been addressed, you must now decide whether your car needs:

• Scratch repairs, colour-restoring and polishing.
• Just colour-restoring and polishing.
• Only polishing.
• No more work, as the paintwork is fine.

Your skills and the paintwork's condition are likely to significantly influence your decision. Other factors to take into account include the purpose of your make-over, your available time, the car's age, and costs, although tasks explained in this chapter should be relatively cheap, unless a scratch repair goes wrong.

If you decide to repair scratches, this should be undertaken before colour-restoring, with polishing done last.

Scratches come in all different shapes and sizes, and so to simplify things, I've split them into three types, depending on repair method.

Repairing minor scratches, which

I'll call grade one, with colour-restorer or more abrasive scratch remover should be simple, and should only rarely go wrong. The same method can be used for surface smudges, marks, exhaust stains, and tar spots.

Repairing deeper scratches, grades two and three, is far more difficult. Think hard before undertaking such work, as you can damage the paintwork. The newer the car the better the scratch repair should be, and the more likely it is that grade two and three scratches should be repaired professionally.

Sometimes, just using colour-restorer or scratch remover – as for a grade one repair – may be enough to sufficiently improve a grade two or grade three scratch, rather than risk a more difficult repair.

The thickness of the car's paint, its hardness, and the shape, size and structure of the scratch will all affect the degree of success achieved by your repairwork. Some repairs will make paintwork look perfect; many repairs will enhance it significantly, but leaving the scratch still just visible; other repairs will be an improvement, but leave blemishes; and if the paint or laquer are fractured, respraying may be the only remedy.

Unfortunately, in some cases, you can cause fresh damage. Even if this happens, the car may still look better with the scratch's visibility diminished, especially, once the area has been colour-restored and polished.

On the other hand, bad damage can be worse than leaving the scratch as it was. So, for many people it may be better to stick to grade one repairs, colour-restoring, and polishing.

If paintwork panels are flat (have lost their shine) and faded, and have just light scratching, such as bush marks, they can usually be enhanced by colour-restoring. Paintwork with worse

blemishes, for example with scratches which you may be wary of trying to repair, can also, normally, be improved by colour-restoring.

You can colour-restore just a panel or two, if they're in a worse condition than the rest of the paintwork, but it's best to do the whole car to get the most even finish.

Colour-restoring liquid compounds or pastes are slightly abrasive, so be careful using them. They improve paintwork by removing built-up residues and an oxidized layer. They also smooth the surface of the paintwork. Fine particles in the restorer gradually break down as it's rubbed in, but using excessive force, for example by rubbing too hard in one direction, can cause fine scratching.

There are a variety of products available to improve paintwork, and they have a variety of characteristics (some include polish) and varying degrees of abrasiveness. They are called scratch removers, colour or paint cutters, colour-restorers, renovators, rubbing compounds, and rubbing pastes. Some are known by their brand names, such as T-Cut and Color Back.

Scratch remover is specifically designed to repair scratches, but colour-restorer and some other similar products may also work, though could take longer.

If you're repairing only a few minor scratches, it may make sense to use just a colour-restorer, rather than buying a scratch repairer as well.

For simplicity's sake I will just use the term 'colour-restore,' but choose a product that's best suited for your task. Colour-cutting pastes may be more abrasive than liquid paint cleaners.

Polishing a car, especially after a colour-restore, will really sharpen up its appearance, particularly if it's got non-metallic paintwork. It should also make it easier to clean in future, and make it look good for longer.

However, none of this work may be needed (if you're lucky), as paintwork on many modern cars is so resilient that it may already be sparkling to your satisfaction.

Before starting any work, it's advisable to read the whole chapter, to understand the various techniques.

Scratches

The first option, and by far the most difficult, is repairing scratches. This can result in glorious paintwork, some improvement, or heart-rending failure. Take care, and don't overreach yourself. The different types of scratches are:

• Grade one – a superficial scratch which has barely gone into the laquer (a clear coat over the base colour), if at all. These scratches can normally be repaired by colour-restoring and then polishing.

• Grade two – a deeper scratch which has gone into the laquer, but not completely through it. It will need very fine rubbing down of the adjoining paintwork, before colour-restoring and then polishing.

• Grade three – a scratch which has gone completely through the laquer to the base layer paint, primer or metal. It will need touching-in, flattening, colour-restoring and polishing.

But how do you identify different scratches?

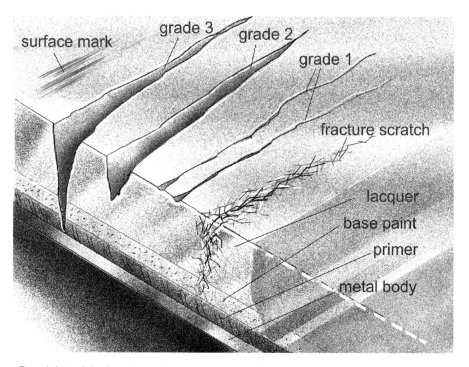

From left-to-right: A mark on the paintwork; grade three scratch; grade two scratch; grade one scratches; and a fracture scratch.

Grade one scratch.

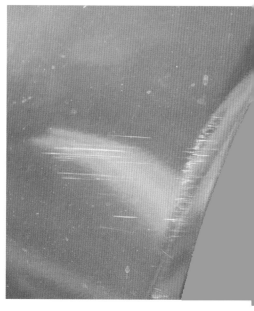

Multiple grade two scratches.

Grade one scratches usually look superficial, on the surface, and you may hardly be able to feel them. They tend to show up white, unless dirty, because they reflect light differently than unblemished paintwork. They may disappear if you wet them, but will reappear when dry.

Grade two scratches are similar to grade ones, but are generally a deeper V or U shape in the laquer, and also normally show up white. You should be able to feel a grade two scratch by running your fingernail gently across it. A grade two scratch will still be slightly visible when wet.

Grade three scratches are deeper, should catch your nail more, and are often a different shade/colour than the surrounding paintwork (depending on whether or not it's gone through to the primer or metal).

You must now assess the importance of improving a scratch, or

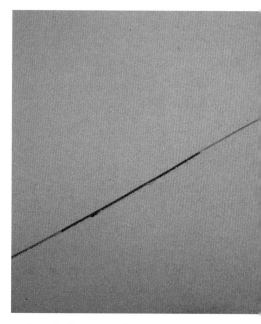

A grade three scratch which has gone through the laquer onto darker paint.

scratches, balanced against the risks of causing further damage.

Many cars can be sold with scratches, and you should be able to improve most of them, to some degree, just using colour-restorer. If you're keeping your car, you may not be bothered by a few scratches.

Alternatively, you may decide that some scratches, particularly bigger ones and those on a new car, should be repaired. Scratches on upward-facing paintwork, including the bonnet and the tops of wings, tend to be more noticeable, so you may be keener to repair them, than those at the bottom of a door.

If you have limited DIY skills, you may already have opted to use a bodywork shop, dentman, or scratch removal expert, though always bear in mind the costs.

As mentioned earlier, if you decide that a panel needs repainting at a bodywork shop, you could try tackling its scratches yourself first, knowing that if you fail you were always going to spend money getting it repaired anyway.

Difficult choices may arise with grade two or grade three scratches – especially if they're glaringly obvious, not significantly improved by colour-restoring, and you doubt that it makes economic sense to get them repaired professionally.

For people with limited DIY skills, it can be best to play safe, and just accept your car as it is, but with the impact of the scratch partially diminished by colour-restoring. Even if you regard your DIY skills as good, and be honest with yourself, be realistic about the likely outcome of your work.

TOP TIP: If you attempt a scratch repair, particularly grade two or three, start with one in a less obvious place, in case the process isn't successful.

Caution! Work carefully and check regularly for damage, thus reducing the likelihood of a mishap (which can happen easily, particularly by rubbing down too much).

TOP TIP: Because you'll be focusing so intently on one small area, you're likely to notice any blemishes, no matter how tiny. Take a break, and come back in 15 minutes – you may find you can no longer even see the scratch which was causing you concern.

Some scratches will consist of several grades at once, and are best repaired by starting with the grade three part, then grade two, and finishing with the grade one section – so touching-in, rubbing down along the length of the scratch, then colour-restoring and polishing.

I repair multiple scratches, in the same area using the same methods outlined below for the different types of scratch. So, do Grade 3 scratches first, followed by a general rubbing down over all the scratches if they're close together.

As you rub down, grade one scratches should be improved first, while grade two and grade three scratches will normally need more work. **Caution!** With multiple scratches, the risk of going through the laquer is greater than for single scratches because you're rubbing down more paintwork.

If you're in doubt over whether a scratch is a grade two or grade three, treat it as a grade three (you're less likely to go through the laquer on a grade three).

Darker colours are easier to touch-in than light, particularly metallic cars, which can be difficult to do successfully.

Grade one scratch.

Grade one

Always read the instructions on your colour-restorer or scratch remover. Unless they advise differently:

• Wet and wring out a polishing cloth, preferably 100 per cent cotton, and put on a small amount of colour-restorer.

• Rub in the direction of the scratch, and then in a small circular pattern across and around the scratch, for 30 seconds to a minute.

Colour-restoring a grade one scratch (note that the tape isn't needed for repairs but is used to highlight the area for the book).

A finished grade one scratch repair.

• Don't press too hard, for too long, or rub excessively in one direction, as this could cause fine scratches. Gentle colour-restoring, in a circular motion, should make them disappear.
• Buff up the colour-restored area with a dry cotton cloth, again without pressing too hard.
• Inspect the scratch to see if it's been improved to your satisfaction. If it hasn't, repeat the colour-restoring and buffing up process.
• Once you're happy with the scratch repair, colour-restore again – slightly less firmly this time, and in a wider circular motion on the surrounding paintwork, so the scratch blends in.
• Buff up with a dry polishing cloth.
• Inspect again.

Some grade one scratches will almost completely disappear, but others will always be slightly visible. Polishing will further enhance the paintwork.

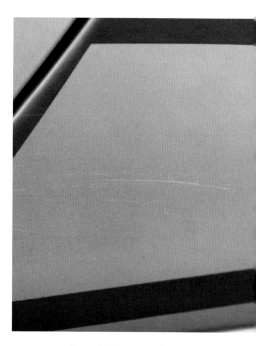

A grade two scratch.

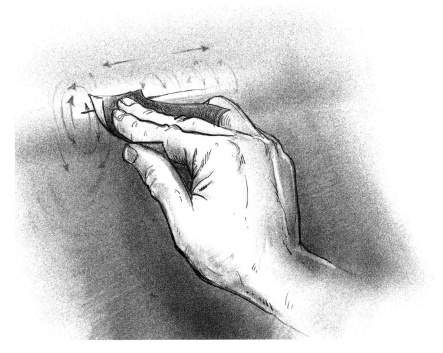

Starting at one end of the scratch, rub gently in a circular motion, going along the scratch. For deeper scratches you can rub up and down the scratch, as indicated by the arrows, and in a circular pattern along it.

Taking a break now can give you a better perspective on your work. However, if you're not getting the required finish, it may be because it is, in fact, a grade two scratch.

Grade two

A grade two scratch is more complicated to repair, and, as you'll be using fine abrasive paper (known as wet-and-dry), there's a greatly increased possibility of damaging the car. Importantly, always check whether grade two, and in particular grade three scratches are also a crease or dent in the metal, made by the pressure that also caused the scratch.

Repairing scratches on concave or flat metalwork can be more difficult than on a convex surface, so you may want to have the dent/crease mended by a dentman, before repairing the scratch yourself, or get a bodyshop to do it all.

If you repair the scratch yourself without getting the dent/crease knocked out, just colour-restore grade two scratches, and touch-in grade three scratches using minimal rubbing down.

TOP TIP: Don't use a rubbing block on concave or flat metalwork, and take extra care not to go through the laquer on such surfaces.

For grade two scratches you'll need very fine wet-and-dry paper (grading 1500 to 2000), a bucket or small tub of water with a dash of washing-up liquid, a tea towel,

Rubbing down with wet-and-dry paper.

colour-restorer, and cotton cloths. Taking great care:

• Dip the wet-and-dry paper in the water, and then rub it very carefully and lightly in a small circular pattern over the scratch and adjoining paintwork, around an inch (2.5cm) either side of the scratch. Start rubbing from just beyond one end of the scratch, working your way along the length of it, and going just beyond the other end. This may be enough rubbing down for minor grade two scratches.

• For deeper scratches, you can carefully and lightly rub in a straight line up and down the scratch, and then again in a circular pattern.

• The aim is to lower the paintwork adjoining the scratch, so the two are closer to being on the same level.

TOP TIP: The scratch and the paintwork don't have to be actually

level – you normally only need to lower the adjoining paintwork part way down to the bottom of the scratch to get a satisfactory finish.

• The big danger is going through the laquer onto the base paint. Stop regularly, clean the scratch area with a damp microfibre cloth, and dry off with a tea towel to check how far down you've gone. You should be able to feel the scratch less and less each time.

• It's best to avoid thinning the paintwork too close to the bottom of the scratch, because, if you do, it can dramatically increase the likelihood of breaking through the laquer onto the paint, which can happen quickly.

Paint normally comes off more easily than laquer.

• If paint comes off – your paper may show colour – you've gone too deep, so stop immediately. Finish off by gently colour-restoring and polishing, seeking to

Rubbed down scratch areas will appear matt, so will need colour-restoring.

A completed grade two scratch repair.

avoid further damage. Badly-damaged paintwork may need respraying.

• After you've slightly thinned the paintwork towards the level of the bottom of the scratch, colour-restore the scratch area; this can take a while as the paintwork will be matt. Let it dry, and then buff up with a dry cloth.

• Inspect your repair, and decide whether you're happy with it. If it's borderline, a polish may help you to make up your mind. Also, a break now could give you a better perspective on your work.

• The scratch may not have completely disappeared, but should be significantly improved already. You might not be able to feel it, but you may still see it, especially if it scarred or fractured the paint underneath.

• If it's almost to your satisfaction, but not sufficiently, you may want a second or third colour-restore, before a final polish.

• If there's still some way to go, you might want to repeat the whole process – but again take special care; you've already taken off some laquer.

• You have to use your judgement when to stop, rather than take further risks of damage.

Grade three

Grade three repairs can take longer as you have to build up paint in the scratch, which can require applying three, four or even more layers.

Clean the scratch, but don't rub down, colour-restore, or polish it, as the touch-in paint will grip better onto a rough surface. If you rub down the area the scratch may lose its V or U shape, making it difficult or impossible to fill. Remember the earlier advice about repairing scratches on concave and flat surfaces.

So, to repair a grade three scratch you need a touch-up stick of the right colour, preferably made by the car

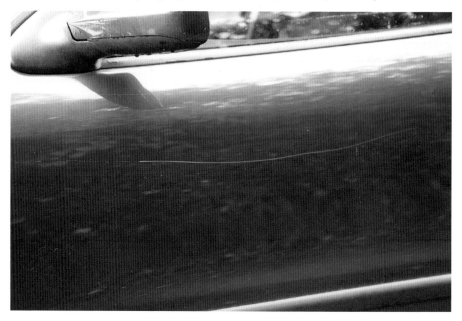

A long grade three scratch spoiling the appearance of the door.

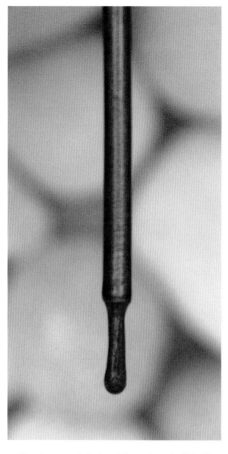

Touch-up paint should create a half-ball shape on the brush, but not a full drop.

becoming a full drop. You want paint to transfer easily into the scratch when you touch it.

• Carefully dab the paint into the scratch, trying to roll it along the scratch and to the edges, but without going over the sides. You're aiming to get the paint to fill the scratch. It's likely to shrink into the scratch as it dries, so don't worry if it's initially slightly proud of

Dabbing in a grade three scratch.

manufacturer, a wet-and-dry rubbing block (preferably made out of cork or rubber) for convex surfaces, wet-and-dry paper, colour-restorer, polish, and cotton cloths.
• Unless the instructions say otherwise, shake the touch-up stick for at least a minute, unscrew the lid, and pull out the touch-up brush.

TOP TIP: Load enough paint on the brush end to form a rounded shape around the bottom, but without

it. Dab or touch-in the paint. Don't use the brush as a paintbrush, going up and down the scratch with paint strokes.
• It's difficult to stop paint building up over the scratch edges, but try to keep this to the minimum. Touch-ins should look tidy, and several attempts may be needed to achieve this, so wipe off the paint with a clean rag and start again until you are satisfied.
   It can be trickier to neatly dab paint in scratches on upward facing surfaces, as the paint tends to come off the brush more quickly.

TOP TIP: If you dab on too much metallic paint, the metallic elements can sink down, leaving a non-metallic finish.

• Sometimes, you need just one layer of paint to fill the scratch, and if your work is very neat you may not need to do anything else.
• Normally, though, you'll need several layers, and have to rub down the paint, especially if it's gone over the edges. Rubbing down is done after the final layer has dried.
• Wait between layers for the previous coat to be properly touch dry, but not fully set.
• In the heat of summer this can take less than half an hour, but in winter it can take far longer.

TOP TIP: It's best to let paint dry in direct sunlight, but don't apply in direct sunlight because the paint can swiftly become tacky.

• Once you've applied the final coat of paint, and the scratch is level or slightly proud of the surrounding paintwork, let it dry properly (this can take a few hours). Don't let it fully harden, though, it has to be easy to rub down, without flaking, and not so hard that it will need lots of rubbing down, thus increasing the risk of going through the laquer.
• Carefully rub down to the level of the surrounding paintwork, using a rubbing block covered with 1500 or 2000 grade wet-and-dry paper. If it's a flat or concave area, use wet-and-dry paper, but not the block.

TOP TIP: Wet-and-dry paper is most abrasive when first used, and can take off paint and laquer quickly. **Caution!** Don't use other abrasive papers, such as sandpaper or sanding blocks.

• Check regularly that you're rubbing down the scratch towards the

Rubbing down a touched-in grade three scratch.

A sparkling door after a grade three scratch repair.

paintwork's level, and that you're not going through the surrounding laquer. Wipe down the scratch area with a damp microfibre cloth, and dry it off with the tea towel, to see, and feel, how your work is progressing.
• Once you have a reasonably even surface, with a matt finish, colour-restore it.
• Stand back and inspect it. You're aiming for a significant improvement, but don't be disappointed if it's not perfection.
• Another short break could give you a better perspective on your work.

If you feel it's good enough, polish the area, otherwise repeat the rubbing down process, but be extremely careful about penetrating through the laquer.

The success of touch-in repairs varies significantly. All repairs, though, should mean that the scratch is less of a scar marring your car's appearance.

Stonechips
Stonechips can be repaired using the same grading system; and they're often easier than scratches to touch-in.

TOP TIP: Sometimes, touching-in may produce a sufficient improvement that you don't have to rub down and colour-restore.

Colour-impregnated polishes can smarten up panels with very fine stonechips, particularly bonnets, though I find they have varying degrees of effectiveness. I prefer to use a home-made polish.

Colour-matching a polish to your car may also be difficult, but a black colour polish may fade fine stonechips into dark paintwork.

Rust
Most modern cars don't have major rust problems, so what follows is merely

a brief overview of how to deal with superficial rust on edges, scratches and stonechips. More severe rust, including rust bubbles, can be treated with specialist anti-rust products before touching-in, but in some cases it may need to be repaired by a bodyshop.

Rust staining may come off with colour-restorer. If it doesn't, a rust remover and some other acid-based products should work. Many of them will need to be diluted, though. **Caution!** Given that these products come with different acid concentrations, it's hard to specify by how much they should be diluted. So, you should get advice when buying a product as to whether it's suitable to remove rust staining on paintwork. Check the instructions, and test it on a non-prominent area of your car first.

Unless instructions say otherwise, rust stained edges can be cleaned with a toothbrush dipped in your chosen product; you can use a cloth or soft paintbrush for rust-stained panels. Swiftly rinse off the acid-based solution, or other products, as instructed, and dry with a cloth or tea towel. Suitable protective gear should be worn (as per when cleaning wheels with acid-based cleaner).

The source of rust staining should also be addressed with an appropriate anti-rust product.

Rusty stonechips, scratches, and other minor rust spots can be cleaned in the same way, before touching-in with a rust treatment, and then with paint. For very minor rust spots on modern cars, you may not actually need to use rust treatment.

TOP TIP: The area must be completely dry so you don't seal in water under the paint.

Rust staining running down the plastic rear bumper.

Colour-restoring a faded wing.

Tar

Tar may accumulate, particularly on wheelarches. It may come off with polish, white spirit or specific tar remover.

Colour-restoring

Colour-restoring is recommended if panels are faded, flat, or have superficial scratches.

Upward-facing surfaces are more likely to be flat than side facing ones. Flatness also tends to be more noticeable on dark cars.

If you're unsure whether your car needs colour-restoring, try polishing one area, and see what happens.

If it sounds or feels rough when polishing it, if it's difficult to get the polish off, or the paintwork seems to absorb polish, it may mean that you need to colour-restore the area.

Bonnets are normally the hardest to colour-restore because the paintwork

is subjected to the engine's heat and is exposed to the elements – and this is the area I tend to start on.

So, unless the instructions say otherwise, apply a large coin-sized amount of colour-restorer onto a damp cotton cloth, and rub it onto the paintwork in a circular pattern – around eight to ten inches wide (20cm to 25cm) – before also rubbing horizontally and vertically. To allow the colour-restorer to work properly, rub it for around a minute on each section measuring around 14 to 16 square inches (35 to 40 square cm).

TOP TIP: Always keep cloths clean, especially grit-free, when colour-restoring or polishing, otherwise you risk scratching the paintwork.

Don't let colour-restorer get too dry as it will become harder to get off. Buff up with a dry cotton cloth, using similar

A colour-restored wing.

motions to those used when applying the restorer.

TOP TIP: Don't mix colour-restoring, buffing up, and polishing cloths.

Some colour-restorers can be washed off with the hose/brush, before drying the area with a microfibre cloth, tea towel or a chamois leather.

Bonnets and other large panels can be colour-restored in strips – but make sure they overlap slightly, so you don't miss any paintwork.

Colour-restore one or two panels at a time, depending on how quickly you're working, and the conditions.

Work your way around the car, and make sure you get into all gaps around badges, lights, mirrors, door handles, chrome grilles etc ... You can put restorer onto a soft toothbrush to work into tight areas, before wiping off any excess with a cotton cloth, and the cleaned toothbrush, and leaving it to dry. You can finish off by buffing up with the cloth and another soft, totally clean toothbrush.

Polish the car after colour-restoring it. Colour-restored panels should keep their shine for longer than those that have just been polished.

If colour-restorer is difficult to get off, use polish to remove it, and then buff up afterwards.

TOP TIP: Colour-restorer can be used to brighten up faded numberplates and plastic light covers.

Chrome and shiny metal exhaust finishers are colour-restored last, using the same methods; this task may require persistence.

Polishing
Polishing should be pretty straightforward, and, like colour-

restoring, should be done out of direct sunlight. You need an appropriate car polish and two polishing cloths (cotton).

Unless the instructions say differently, pour a large coin-size amount of polish onto a damp cloth, and apply in a circular pattern on one section, such as a wing, rubbing it in vertically and horizontally as well. Let it dry to a haze and then buff up with a dry cloth.

Working around the car, you should find that other panels, the bonnet, and roof should be easy to polish, but make sure you also do edges and other harder-to-access areas to give your car an all-over shine. Polish residue in tight areas can be removed with a paintbrush if needed.

TOP TIP: Take care when polishing freshly-painted panels as they can scratch more easily.

Trim

When colour-restoring paintwork, you'll almost certainly get polish and colour-restorer on black trim, such as bumper strips, grilles, rubbing strips, door handles, mirror surrounds, window seals and tyres.

TOP TIP: Completely cleaning these products off trim can be finicky, but it's crucial to do so for the finest finish.

Colour-restorer on trim may rub off with a cloth, but applying polish can help to remove it. Polish can often, also, be rubbed off with a cloth.

If these methods don't work, try using a nailbrush or toothbrush, and soap. If this is unsuccessful, you can resort to special trim cleaner.

Trim finisher can also be used to improve the appearance of trim, but make sure you work it into all gaps and creases, as missed areas will stand out. Trim finishers with dye, usually black, work well. I prefer finishers without silicon.

Wheels can be polished, but it's often best to colour-restore them first.

six
Photos and adverts

Kit
Camera, computer.

Estimated time: one hour.
Goal: Attracting buyers.
Sale booster factor: ☆☆☆☆.

As photographs will convey the first impression that many viewers will get of a car, it's crucial to get high quality shots. Well-taken pictures show cars in their full glory, whereas close-up, front-on mug shots can make them look plain ugly.

Light
You don't need an expensive camera. A reasonable quality camera, preferably one on which you can manually alter the exposure setting – ie, increase the light entering the camera (by enlarging the aperture, slowing the shutter speed, or both) – compared to the automatic setting which can leave cars under-exposed, should be fine.

TOP TIP: Slightly over-exposing photos of a car's exterior should display its colour, details and definition so the picture stands out in comparison to others.

Some automatic cameras can be tricked into over-exposure by pointing them at darker areas, which are the same distance from your car, half-pressing and holding down the button, pointing the camera back at the vehicle, and then fully pressing down the button to take the picture.
Increase the exposure for light-coloured cars more than dark models.
Do the interiors on standard exposure, unless they're light-coloured, in which case you can slightly increase the exposure as well. If you have bright backgrounds, such as a bright sky, you may have to over-expose the picture more, so the car doesn't look too dark. Gloomy pictures not only give a negative impression, but often you can't properly see the car.

Gleaming car in an ideally exposed picture.

Cars tend to look dull when shot on automatic exposure.

73

TOP TIP: Using a flash can make cars look dark and scruffy.

I always take a series of shots to get at least four good photos: two exterior; two interior. You can take more pictures of different sections and angles of the car, but I regard four as key:

- The driver's side, taking in the front.
- The passenger's side, taking in the rear.
- The driver's seat.
- The passenger's seat or rear seats.

However, before you start your photoshoot, think about the timing and location.

Weather
The weather, type of sunlight, time of day, background, and angles are all crucial to the quality of photographs.

TOP TIP: Cloudy but bright days, I find, are best for pictures. You get a nice even light which gives well-defined photos.

If it's a sunny day, especially in the summer, it's best to take the pictures in the shade, early morning, or late afternoon, as it's more difficult to get good pictures in direct or bright sunlight.

Winter pictures are often best taken during the brightest part of the day; while in spring and autumn, it all depends on the weather, which can be so variable.

TOP TIP: Photographs with fallen leaves, or snow, may become dated if the weather changes. So, you may then have to do a new set.

Background
Ideally, you want a consistent background – like a well-kept hedge, an attractive wall, a screen of trees or an open space. Consistency in backgrounds lets your car take centre stage.

Dirty streets, litter-strewn pavements, and walls with crumbling brickwork are dreadful backgrounds.

This dull, under-exposed picture is also dated by the snow.

An evergreen hedge will mean the picture shouldn't date.

Dirty walls, dirty car, fragmented background and hanging washing spoil the picture.

A clean-cut background – and a clean car – enhances the photo.

TOP TIP: Even on a normal street, a front-on picture of a car, taken from two metres away, is likely to be a poor photograph.

Not all backgrounds have to be bland. Cars can also look good in front of an ornate gateway, an elegant house, or on a sweeping driveway.

TOP TIP: Dynamic backgrounds, such as clean-cut steel structures, can add vibrancy to a picture, and are particularly suitable for sports cars and other rare models.

But you don't want to appear to be trying too hard, or seeking to use the background to make your car seem better than it is. You are, after all, selling a car, not entering a photographic competition.

Main picture
The most important picture is the front, driver's side, diagonal shot.
Stand back six to seven metres (18 to 21 feet), any closer than this and

the car will appear distorted. Adjust the zoom to take a picture showing the front, and also the whole of the driver's side. The latter should take up around three quarters of the photo. This side is the most interesting as people can imagine getting into the car.

TOP TIP: Your car should fill the picture frame, almost touching the photo's front and back edges, so people can see as much of the car as possible.

If you take a picture mainly of the front, you'll fill the photo, but the vehicle may look squat and square. Taking it from the side may make it look sleeker, but you'll see less of the vehicle. A diagonal shot should display more of your car, and at an attractive angle.

Rear diagonal shot
The second, exterior picture is the rear/ passenger's side diagonal shot. Again, the photo aims to capture around three quarters of the car's side and a quarter of the rear. Together, the two exterior shots should display your entire car.

Three quarters of the main picture is taken up by the side.

Diagonal rear shot, which, with the main picture, shows off the whole car in two photos.

TOP TIP: Taking a picture from the side makes some models, such as Porsches, look funky, low and sleek.

You'll have to stand further back for this picture, around nine metres (27 feet) for many cars, so you'll waste vertical space on the photo.

Behind the wheel

A picture of the driver's seat is essential. There are two main ways to take such a photo. The first is from around two metres (six feet) away from the car, and standing a step or two to the rear of the opened door, so you're looking slightly

77

Sleek and beautiful Porsche.

Sideways-on shot of the driver's seat.

forward into the vehicle. The photo should show most of the door opening and the seat, the pedals, most if not all of the dashboard, and the centre console.

Alternatively, get into the car's back seat and take a picture over the driver's seat, over its inside shoulder, or through the headrest. It should show the steering wheel, the pedals, the centre

Driver's seat seen from the rear.

console, but not the far passenger side of the dashboard. You should be able to get in the gearstick. This picture should display the car's cleanliness at close quarters, and allow people to imagine driving it.

The fourth photo shows off the passenger seat or rear seats. It's best to do both and choose the best one.

Front passenger seat
To take the picture of the front passenger seat, stand more square-on to the car than you did for the photo of the driver's side, because there are no pedals to show off. From this angle, your photo should show the car's breadth, including the driver's seat.

TOP TIP: The front passenger seat picture looks good if it has a wide

Passenger seat, looking across the car.

Rear seats, looking forward slightly.

sweep across the car, even taking in the far edge of the driver's seat.

Rear seat

For the rear seat, you want a picture across the car, looking slightly forward. The door may restrict how square-on you can get.

With three-door cars, move one front seat forward, as far as possible, before tipping it forward. Then try to capture in a diagonal shot as much of the rear seats as you can.

If you're doing more than four photos (some websites allow many more), you can include the boot, the engine, a close-up of a wheel, all the interior shots mentioned above, square on photos, and four rather than two diagonal, exterior pictures.

Photos can make some imperfections look worse than they're. For example, if you've had a wing painted, the slight colour difference may

Driver's seat tipped forward to allow a view of the rear seat.

appear more pronounced in a picture.

By changing the angle of a photo of

Sports cars can look good from above or the side.

a resprayed wing, you can often make it blend in more. You're not trying to fool potential buyers, but you don't want to make it look worse than it actually is.

On a similar note, the camera can sometimes make tyres look brown and more tired than they are. Spraying the wheelarches and tyres with water, with a drop of washing-up liquid in, should improve definition.

Overall, I tend to take a few dozen photos, with varying exposure adjustments and angles, and select the best.

You can stand on a chair, around four metres (12 feet) away, to take pictures of sports cars and convertibles.

TOP TIP: Don't fall off! Your sense of balance can desert you when looking through a camera.

Advertising

Decide how to advertise your car. Advertising has been greatly affected by new technology and the changing media and internet landscape, and this is likely to continue. Cars can be advertised on the internet, in motoring magazines, local, regional or national newspapers, or by putting up a notice in your car, a local shop, or on other notice boards. Check out the different rates for adverts, and try to get an idea of how many people will see them.

TOP TIP: Adverts are greatly improved with a picture.

The motoring sections of classified advert websites are an inexpensive, sometimes even free, way to advertise, and can be good for cheap cars.

Websites and magazines specifically for car sales may be more expensive to advertise in, though some may also be free. They can generate more interest, especially for middle-priced and more expensive vehicles. The more exclusive, distinctive and expensive your car is, the more likely it is that you want to find a specialist site to advertise it – a sports car site for a sporty model, or a vintage motoring site for an old treasure.

Advertising cars in local

Mini Cooper Clubman 1.6 diesel manual 5-door 2009 33,000 miles.
Chilli red with black roof and mirrors, black and Rooster Red part leather interior, sport seats, Chilli pack: Pace 17 inch alloy wheels, TLC (pre-paid service pack), climate control, A/C, cruise control, multi function steering wheel. Bought from our local Mini main dealer who serviced it. Red and black together look fantastic. Just had two new front tyres. Recently MoTed and serviced. Always been garaged and never damaged. 50mpg easily attainable. A lovely car that will be much missed. (Price).

newspapers is likely to be cheaper than in regional or national papers, but you'll probably not reach such a wide readership. The more expensive your car is, the wider you may need to search for a buyer.

Be concise when writing your advertising copy, so you pack as much information as you can into a small number of words. First, list the basics, including make, model, engine size, type (hatchback, saloon, estate or convertible), fuel, whether it's manual or automatic, age and mileage. The specification autofill on some websites may need to be overridden so you can use your own wording.

Next, mention the exterior and interior colour, including the type of seats (if they are leather or other special material), before listing the most important optional extras and standard equipment. These can include air-conditioning, climate control, the navigation system, heated seats, cruise control, a power roof, audio systems, and any special wheels. Don't forget to include the price.

TOP TIP: A good advert should feel personal, so you can include such details as length of ownership, whether it's been in the family from new, if it's in original condition, always been garaged and proved reliable.

The service history, MoT length, and any recent work, such as new tyres or brakes, should also be included. It can be better to say 'long MoT,' rather than 'ten months' MoT,' in case the car takes a while to sell.

TOP TIP: Don't undersell the car; but equally don't over-advertise it as better than it is, as this is only likely to lead to disappointment for potential buyers, wasting their and your precious time.

seven
Selling techniques

Kit
Good manner, tidy appearance and patience.

Estimated time: Up to 40 minutes per viewing.
Goal: Selling the car.
Sale booster factor: ✰✰ to ✰✰✰.

Super-slick salesmen may be able to sell a dud car for a high price, but this book is not about such dodgy practices. Instead, it aims to make your super-clean car essentially sell itself. My best selling methods, very much in order of importance, are as follows:

- Make your car look stunning.
- Take good photos, to show it in its best light.
- Attract viewers with a personalized advert.
- Do your best to sell the car.

Now, falling in love with a car can take seconds. Beautiful curves, a sparkling personality and an aura of reliability can have a buyer smitten almost instantly. On the other hand, a prospective purchaser may initially show little enthusiasm. Gradually, though, a car's appeal can grow on people as they get to know it, and realise their limited finances restrict what they can honestly expect to buy. Whichever it is, buying a car is a big decision, and often comes down to a car winning over an individual's heart and mind, so they like and trust it to serve them well for years to come.

Great expectations
There's a danger, though, that expectations are so high that people can easily have them shattered. So, any sale should be carefully planned. To start with, be positive, honest, and don't oversell on the phone.

TOP TIP: When someone makes an appointment to see your car, ask them for a phone number, so you can call them if they don't turn up, rather than just waiting in, sometimes in vain, for them to come.

When they do arrive, viewers will only be disappointed, and potentially put off, if they feel that a vehicle is not what it was billed as – which takes us straight to the nub of selling – trust.

Trust

If potential buyers like you, it will make your selling job easier. If they believe you're dishonest, then you face an uphill struggle. So, remember your conduct can influence a sale.

A pile of documents can inspire trust in a car and the seller.

First impressions are important given the short time you're likely to spend with a viewer. If you answer the door in a dirty string vest, unshaven, cigarette hanging out of your mouth and with the dog growling, that nice couple who have come to see your car may swiftly turn on their heels.

You need to be presentable, while also being wary of the risks of over-dressing. Wearing your smartest suit or dress could arouse suspicions that you're trying to pass off your car as better than it really is.

Records of a car's upkeep, including MoT certificates, preferably dating back years, an up-to-date service book and receipts of work carried out can also help to gain a viewer's trust. Make sure the service book is fully stamped. If you've lost servicing or work receipts, you should be able to get duplicate copies. The MoT history can also be found online.

Buyers

All prospective buyers are different. You may get a viewing from Miss Impulsive, Mr Cautious, Mr and Mrs Realistic (if you're lucky), or Mr and Mrs Cloud-Cuckoo-Land. Try to work out how best to treat them individually. Are you giving them enough attention? Taking other calls about your car and not focusing on the sale risks annoying some viewers. Other people, though, may be encouraged into a purchase if they know you may soon have more offers.

Are you giving them enough space? After people have seen a car, they may want time by themselves to mull over whether or not to buy it. They may be too embarrassed to ask to be alone, so it can be best to offer them some privacy.

TOP TIP: Keep the keys yourself to stop anyone driving off with the car, or inadvertently leaving with them in their pocket.

Positives

As viewers inspect your car, it's crucial to highlight what's best about it, including any aspects that might particularly appeal to them.

TOP TIP: Making a list of these good points in advance can be very helpful when it comes to accentuating the positives. They could include that:

- It has only done 30,000 miles.
- It's in excellent condition for its age.
- It has a low fuel consumption.
- 'My wife has had it from new.'
- It's got heated, ventilated seats.
- It has a full service history, and has never broken down.
- It has a sunroof, hi-tech stereo system and alloy wheels.
- It's well priced.

Secondhand cars, though, by their very nature, will have some flaws, but you should try not to sound as if you're giving excuses.

TOP TIP: You want to exude as much confidence as possible about your car. If you display a lack of confidence, the viewer may have nagging doubts.

Faults

If you find yourself having to explain a list of faults, you're detracting from your key aim of trumpeting your car's good points, which you may only have ten or less minutes to do.

TOP TIP: You should be aware of your car's shortcomings, and be able to explain them briefly to a viewer.

A list can again be helpful, and could include that:

- Unevenly worn tyres are normally due to the wheel alignment, which can be easily fixed.
- Minor scratches can be easily repaired.
- While the mileage is high, it has had only two careful owners and has a full service history.

Sometimes, a prospective buyer may, initially, be standoffish and seem to want to find fault with your car. That challenging attitude often mellows, but

you can't satisfy everyone, so don't take every rejection to heart.

Even minor damage can scupper some sales. For some individuals cars are a status symbol, and they can regard a small imperfection on a vehicle as almost a slur on themselves. It could be a scratch, a slightly faded patch on a wing, or a nick in a seat which they know will be a constant irritation. This seems to be particularly the case for men buying sports cars and other exclusive models.

Difficult friend

Most cars are still bought by men, whether it's for themselves, their wife, partner, parents or children, and one obstacle sometimes encountered is the 'difficult friend.' He (and it normally is a man) arrives with a viewer and thinks he knows, and he may actually know, a lot about cars. He may feel he has to demonstrate his motoring knowledge, by finding faults with your car ... even some that don't exist. The way to deal with the 'difficult friend' – and buyers generally – is to be able to answer all their questions. The more you know about your car, the better prepared you'll be.

TOP TIP: While being polite, directing your answers to the buyer, not the 'friend,' may diminish his influence.

Pointing out a couple of items that might need checking or seeing to later – such as wheel alignment – will also give the impression that you're not trying to pull the wool over a buyer's eyes.

Often, you get more than one person coming for a viewing. You can initially focus on the person who likes your car most, to encourage their interest. However, you also need to persuade the person who will hand over the money. So, for a father and his son or daughter, it may be the younger generation that's first attracted to your car, but it could be their parent who you need to convince that it's being sold at a proper price and is likely to be reliable.

Test drive

If people are serious about buying a car, they're likely to ask for a test drive. If people seem to be in two minds about a purchase, you can even suggest a test drive, which sometimes proves to be a decisive factor.

Choosing a suitable test route in advance is advisable, preferably without too many traffic jams. Ideally, you want a route that allows the viewer to put a car through its paces, going up through the gears, before getting onto a stretch of more open road to feel the car purring along, combined with a few bends. Flat routes, with easy-to-drive roads, are best, as viewers may be slightly nervous negotiating tight bends or steep hills. Motorways or other major trunk roads tend not be good choices, as you can end up stuck on them for a while.

TOP TIP: Avoid roads with noisy surfaces, as people may think it's the car making worrying sounds.

Safety considerations should include trying to make sure that a viewer is not going to drive off with your vehicle (normally a rare occurrence), and not putting yourself at risk. If you're a woman selling a car, it may be better to get your husband or a male friend to take people on test drives.

TOP TIP: Make sure you have enough fuel. If the fuel warning light is on, the viewer is unlikely to enjoy the drive.

Insurance

It's important to think about insurance

arrangements, including whether the viewer's insurance covers your car, but even if it does it's likely to only be third party. Likewise, you should consider how to accept payment for a car, so you actually get the money. This general advice is offered as matters which you should address, but this book is not a guide on contractual law, insurance, potential losses and liabilities, financial transactions or any other legal issues. If you want such advice, you should seek it from a legal or other expert.

Price

Researching your car's value, by looking for similar or almost identical cars on motor sales websites or in motoring magazines, should give you a ballpark figure of what yours could fetch. Make sure you're comparing like-for-like, though, taking into account all of your car's major optional extras; or lack of them.

Having cleaned your car properly, as explained in this book, aim to sell it for between what the average private individual and the average trader are seeking. There's no guarantee that you'll achieve this, but that should be your goal.

Traders will demand more because they'll offer a warranty, of course, and should have checked the condition of the vehicle. Private individuals can purchase their own warranties, which can be activated at the point of sale, but you need to work out whether doing so would make economic sense.

While deciding on your asking price, make sure you make several comparisons with similar vehicles because they're likely to range from the very cheap to the ridiculously expensive.

TOP TIP: Knowing what similar cars are being sold for should give you the confidence to defend your asking price.

You can also build into the original price an amount by which you're happy to reduce it. However, this could mean that you over-price the car, and attract less interest.

If you're keen to sell quickly, you can price it slightly under the competition locally, if it's a common car, or nationally if it's a rare model. Asking a very low price is likely to spark interest in a car, but it may make people think that there's something wrong with it.

The number of phone calls, or other inquiries that you get should allow you to gauge whether you've correctly priced your car. A flood of calls would suggest it's too cheap, while an ominous silence may mean you're being too ambitious – or it's August or December, and everyone is on holiday or preparing for Christmas.

However, like so many things in life, there's no guarantee that you'll get the price that you're seeking or deserve. There are so many variables when it comes to a sale, including the number of potential buyers, where they live, the competition, the financial climate, your advert, your selling skills ... and, of course, luck.

Timing
Even the time of day, week and year can influence sales. Summer holidays and immediately before Christmas tend to be quieter times for selling cars, with the busier times normally autumn and spring. Convertibles and sports cars can sell better in spring and summer, while four-wheel drives often go for good money in snowy winters.

Weekends and evenings are when most people want to see cars, so being flexible and available at short notice is important as the window of opportunity to clinch a sale can be small. Your viewer may be an impulse buyer, or in desperate need of a new car quickly because the last one has conked out.

Cars may look better in the evening, late afternoon or morning than in bright midday sun, which can highlight scratches and dents, take the depth out of their colour, and bleach their appearance. However, I wouldn't put off a midday viewing just to try to show the car in better light.

In the winter, you'll be limited by the hours of daylight. If people want to see your car after dark, you can often find a lighted area, but again think about safety.

Offers
You could be tempted to accept the first offer, but it may be low. If you hold your nerve, often, but not always, you'll get closer to the price that you're seeking.

TOP TIP: Car prices are colour-sensitive and this tends to go in trends, with silver, blue and white models, for example, fetching good money some years, but other times falling out of favour.

Sometimes, it can take a month or more for a suitable buyer to spot that your car is being advertised. Like buses, sometimes offers don't come for ages, but then two or three turn up at once! People rarely initially offer the asking price, but if they're serious about a purchase they'll normally up their bid.

It may not yet be to your satisfaction, and you can stand your ground by arguing, if true, that other vehicles may be a little cheaper but they're unlikely to be as nice, and plenty will be more expensive. You can also question whether viewers really want to spend more time scouring adverts and going to see more cars, when they can buy yours now.

TOP TIP: Some people will make a startlingly low offer, but this may just be a bargaining tactic to drive you down to a low compromise figure.

People can also be unrealistic when looking at a secondhand car. They sometimes don't accept that they're spending a modest sum for a car that's several years old.

Many of them can be brought down to earth, by talking them through what your car has to offer, explaining how you think it compares favourably to similar cars on the market, and making them realize how much more a newer model would cost.

For buyers seeking a car at a fraction of its real price, you just have to accept that they're probably not the person with whom you want to strike a deal.

If you've priced your car properly, you may still want to be ready to accept a slightly lower figure to seal a deal and give the buyer a sense of satisfaction at having bartered you down. However, don't be bullied into accepting a price which you'll later regret.

TOP TIP: Avoid sounding desperate to sell your car, even if you are, as this is likely to weaken your negotiating position.

Sealing the deal

After all your hard work, be wary of falling for a buyer's bluff.

TOP TIP: If you've cleaned, prepared and priced your car properly, you should be in a good position to defend the sum you're seeking.

Often people will say that the price is more than they want to spend. This may be true. But this is normally the case when individuals are buying a house or a car. In the end, they often stretch their finances as they accept they're unlikely to get a better deal.

Again, holding your nerve can be important. If they like your car, they may want to buy it as much as you want to sell.

If people say they've seen a better car in a bid to barter you down, ask them about the details. You may find it's an older model, with higher mileage, lower specifications, or a dreadful colour scheme. They may not admit that to you, but it could make them rethink their negotiating stance.

Finally, when it comes to the crunch, deals are often struck by one or both parties making a compromise. But any compromise should hopefully be one, over which you'll not lose sleep.

eight
Psychology

Lurking deep within your car, in its every pore and sinew ... is you.

In the most striking example, flecks of dead skin, mixed with sebaceous grease and bacteria, are often found on or around repeatedly-touched objects, such as the gearstick and steering wheel.

And without wishing to get too personal, many cars smell of their owners, their pets, or their work.

Now, to increase your chances of a successful sale it's crucial that you rid your car of ... you.

This is done by thoroughly cleaning it, and removing personal paraphernalia.

Disease
Most cars are dirtier than they appear at first glance, and, since time immemorial, dirt has been closely associated with disease. An evolved protective mechanism imbued in mankind to help avoid threats and ill-fate, can often be triggered by dirty environments without people even seeming to realise. But what has this all got to do with selling a car, you may ask? Well, in the modern world, these basic human instincts still apply, and our cleanliness expectations when it comes to cars can be very high after they've been paraded in glossy magazines and displayed in excruciatingly clean showrooms.

Bad vibes
Years in the car trade have taught me that people may buy or reject a car without appearing to have reached any sound reasoning for doing so. This seems, in some cases, to be down to almost subconscious forces. It may seem mysterious, but even cars in good condition can trigger 'bad vibes,' which can scupper a sale. On the other hand, I've sometimes been left wondering why people have spent a large sum on a car that they've seen for just a matter of minutes.

No matter the quirks and characteristics of prospective buyers, a good make-over seems to diminish the influence of nature's forces.

TOP TIP: Never believe someone who rings up saying: "Don't bother cleaning the car, I'm happy as it is." They almost certainly won't be.

For many people, dirt and minor damage signal that the car hasn't been looked after properly. They may be left thinking: "Has the owner checked the oil regularly? Serviced the car? Thrashed it from cold, speeding up the road?" Therefore, cleanliness is crucial to ensure your car is perceived in the best light.

Ghosts
Removing someone's presence from a car is vital to sell it. Most people want a blank canvas. They don't want the previous owner lingering like a ghost.

TOP TIP: By cleaning a car, you're exorcising yourself from it, leaving it free for someone to step in and take possession. It should shout out: "I'm yours to drive away."

New life
By taking a car back towards its original showroom condition, you're allowing it to tempt the buyer by conveying its new lease of life.
People can become blind to their own grime; potential buyers may have higher expectations of your vehicle than their own.

TOP TIP: Get a friend, neighbour or your partner to give you an honest, second opinion. They may see things which are almost invisible to you.

The truth
So open your eyes fully to your car's true condition.

- Did you notice the layer of dust on the dashboard?
- Whose long, blond hair is that on the passenger's seat?
- And that stale perfume or aftershave on the seatbelt ... yours?
- Do your hands stick to the steering wheel?
- Oh! And that doggy smell?

The list could be endless, but once you see all the glaring, half-obvious and sometimes almost hidden imperfections, you can nearly always clean them away, or at least limit their impact.

Tacky
Many people like buying a car without frills, oddities and peculiarities.

TOP TIP: A good starting point is to think what your car would be like new.

Obviously, that does not mean that a special radio, alloy wheels or other high spec items will not help to sell your car. However, what you may regard as a symbol of great individuality – a favoured sticker, a dashboard shined up with silicon spray, or a pair of fluffy dice – may be dismissed by buyers as tacky.
Big wheels, low suspension and a big exhaust may appeal to boy racers, but to many people they leave the impression of a car that has been hammered on the road. Admittedly, some of your car's individuality may not be easily changed, or certainly not cheaply, but other items can be removed, which will make it appeal to more people, as you prepare it for a new owner.
Emotionally, it can be difficult to let go of a trusted companion after many years. But only once you are gone from the car, at least as far as possible, can it truly start to become 'theirs.'

British/US glossary

British	American
Accelerator	Gas pedal
Anti-clockwise	Counter-clockwise
Bonnet	Hood
Brake disc	Brake disk
Boot	Trunk
Colour	Color
Electric windows/seats	Power windows/seats
Exhaust manifold	Header
Estate car	Station wagon
Indicator	Turn signal
Motorway	Freeway, Interstate
Numberplate	Licence plate
Petrol	Gasoline
Roof rack	Car top carrier
Soft top	Convertible top
Tail gate	Lift gate/tail gate
Saloon/booted car	Sedan
Sills	Rockers
Tea towel	Dish towel
Tyre	Tire
Washing up liquid	Dish washing liquid
Wet and dry paper	Fine water proof sand paper (automotive)
Wing/front	Fender
Wing/rear	Quarter panel
Wheel bolt/nut	Lug bolt/nut
Windscreen	Windshield

ISBN: 978-1-845843-88-5
- Paperback • 21x14.8cm
- £9.99* UK/$19.95* USA • 80 pages
- 115 colour pictures

ISBN: 978-1-845843-51-9
- Paperback • 21x14.8cm
- £9.99* UK/$19.95* USA • 96 pages
- 32 colour pictures

A clean and well-tended car will look better, be more pleasurable to drive, and have a superior resale value. This book is a step-by-step guide to the various elements of car care, from washing, waxing and polishing, to engine cleaning and leather maintenance.

Describes in a clear, friendly manner everything today's driver needs to know about choosing and using a car in an economical and eco-efficient way. Includes helpful information on alternative fuels, hybrid powertrains, and much more.

Also available in eBook format

For more info on Veloce titles, visit our website at www.veloce.co.uk
- email: info@veloce.co.uk • Tel: +44(0)1305 260068
* prices subject to change, p&p extra

Index